2014

Ready® Common Core

Reading Instruction 3

point of view
main idea
character

Curriculum Associates

D1059799

Acknowledgments

Mary Reina, "Teeny Tiny Tardigrades" from *Highlights*, August 2011. Copyright © 2011 by *Highlights* for Children, Inc., Columbus, OH. Reprinted with permission.

"More Ice Would Be Nice" adapted from *Scholastic News*, February 27, 2012. Copyright © 2012 by Scholastic, Inc. Reprinted with permission.

Jennifer R. Hubbard, "A Boy Called Everest" from *Cricket* magazine, January 2012, Volume 39, Number 4. Copyright © 2012 by Jennifer R. Hubbard. Reprinted with permission of Carus Publishing Company.

Dale-Marie Bryan, "An Earful" from *Highlights*, January 2005. Copyright © 2005 by *Highlights* for Children, Inc., Columbus, OH. Reprinted with permission.

Vicky Alvear Shecter, "Cleopatra Finds Her Voice" from *Highlights*, January 2009. Copyright © 2009 by *Highlights* for Children, Inc., Columbus, OH. Reprinted with permission.

Pamela Walker, "Real Treasure" from *Highlights*, January 2011. Copyright © 2011 by *Highlights* for Children, Inc., Columbus, OH. Reprinted with permission.

Natasha Yim, "Horses Helping Others" adapted from *Appleseeds* issue: Horsing Around, May 2011. Copyright © 2011 by Carus Publishing Company. Published by Cobblestone Publishing, 30 Grove Street, Suite C, Peterborough, NH 03458. Reprinted with permission. All rights reserved.

Fran Downey and Peter Winkler, "Crazy Critters" adapted from *National Geographic Explorer*, January-February 2007. Copyright © 2007 by Fran Downey/National Geographic Stock. Reprinted with permission.

Nancy Whitelaw, "Our Most Famous Immigrant" adapted from *Cobblestone* issue: Ellis Island: Gateway to America, February 2006. Copyright © 2006 by Carus Publishing Company. Published by Cobblestone Publishing, 30 Grove Street, Suite C, Peterborough, NH 03458. Reprinted with permission. All rights reserved.

Jennifer Mattox, "Big Bugs" from *Highlights*, October 2009. Copyright © 2009 by *Highlights* for Children, Inc., Columbus, OH. Reprinted with permission.

George Cooper, "The Wind and the Leaves" from *Playtime Stories (Readers)*, Published by First NY American Book Company (1921). Public domain.

Pat Betteley, "How the Animals Got Their Beautiful Coats" adapted from *Faces* issue: Nelson Mandela: Voice of Human Rights, February 2006. Copyright © 2006 by Carus Publishing Company. Published by Cobblestone Publishing, 30 Grove Street, Suite C, Peterborough, NH 03458. Reprinted with permission. All rights reserved.

"Little Puppy," traditional Navajo poem, transcribed by Hilda Faunce Wetheril (1923). Public domain.

Edward Lear, "There Was an Old Man with a Beard" from *A Book of Nonsense* (1846). Public domain.

"Little By Little" by Anonymous, from *Required Poems for Reading and Memorizing*, Published by Third and Fourth Grades, Prescribed by State Courses of Study (1906). Public domain.

Lori Anastasia, "Basketball Ballet" from *Highlights*, December 2009. Copyright © 2009 by *Highlights* for Children, Inc., Columbus, OH. Reprinted with permission.

Mary Ann Hoberman, "Squirrel" from *A Little Book of Beasts*. Copyright © Mary Ann Hoberman. Copyright © 1973 by mary Ann Hoberman. Used by permission of the Gina Maccoby.

Nancy Shepherdson, "Freaky Foods" adapted from *Boys' Life,* 1998. Copyright © 1998 by Nancy Shepherdson. Published by Boy Scouts of America. Reprinted with permission of the author.

Karin Gaspartich, "Patriotic Pizza" from *Highlights*, January 2007. Copyright © 2007 by *Highlights* for Children, Inc., Columbus, OH. Reprinted with permission.

Kacey Hartung, "Writing On a Wasp's Nest" adapted from *Appleseeds* issue: From Papyrus to Pixels–The ABC's of Writing, November 2004. Copyright © 2004 by Carus Publishing Company. Published by Cobblestone Publishing, 30 Grove Street, Suite C, Peterborough, NH 03458. Reprinted with permission. All rights reserved.

Jaime Joyce, "Goodbye, Books?" from *Time for Kids*, November 20, 2009. Copyright © 2009 by Time for Kids. All rights reserved. Used by permission and protected by the Copyright Laws of the United States. The printing, copying, redistribution, or retransmission of this Content without expressed, written permission is prohibited. www.timeforkids.com/

Mary Pope Osborne, "Paul Bunyan" and "Stormalong" from *American Tall Tales*. Copyright © 1991 by Mary Pope Osborne. Used by permission of Alfred A. Knopf, an imprint of Random House Children's Books, a division of Random House, Inc. Any third party use of this material, outside of this publication, is prohibited. Interested parties must apply directly to Random House, Inc., for permission.

Alfred J. Church, Excerpts from "The Home of the Winds," "Of the Sirens and Other Wonders," and "The Cyclops" from *The Odyssey for Boys and Girls*. Copyright © 1906 by The Macmillan Company, New York. Public domain.

Common Core State Standards © Copyright 2010. National Governors Association Center for Best Practices and Council of Chief State School Officers. All rights reserved.

Language Arts Florida Standards (LAFS) © 2014. Florida Department of Education.

All third-party content has been permissioned or is in the process of being permissioned.

Project Manager: Melissa Brown
Cover Designer and Illustrator: Julia Bourque
Book Design: Mark Nodland

Table of Contents

Table of Contents

Language Handbook

Conventions of Standard English

Table of Contents

Do you think it would be fun to be a reporter? You'd get to write interesting news stories. How would you get the facts for these stories? You would ask questions and look for the answers. You would want to find out what happened, where it happened, and who it happened to. Next, you'd figure out when it happened. And finally, you'd figure out why it happened. In this way, a reporter is like a good reader.

In this unit, you'll learn to ask good questions and look for the answers. You'll read about events in history and see how one event leads to another. You'll read about kinds of weather, and learn how one event can cause another. These skills will help you become a better reader. Who knows, you may become a good reporter, too!

✓ Self Check

Before starting this unit, check off the skills you know below. As you complete each lesson, see how many more you can check off!

I know how to:	Before this unit	After this unit
ask and answer questions about what I read.	☐	☐
find the main idea and important details of a passage.	☐	☐
look for words that show time order.	☐	☐
find connections between ideas in a passage.	☐	☐
look for why things happened in a passage.	☐	☐

Asking Questions About Key Ideas

CCSS
RI.3.1: Ask and answer questions to demonstrate understanding of a text, referring explicitly to the text as the basis for the answer.

Theme: *Animal Homes*

We **ask questions** to get information about something. A question often begins with *who, what, where, when, why,* or *how.* When you answer a question, it's important to show how and where you found the answer.

In the picture, make four question marks next to things you want to ask about.

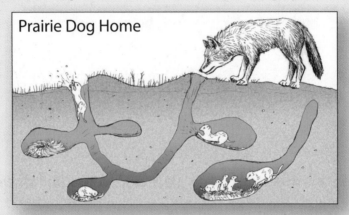

Prairie Dog Home

Now read the table below to see how you can ask questions to get information. Fill in the last row with one of your own questions, a detail from the picture that helps you answer the question, and your answer.

Question	Details from Picture	Answer
What are most of the animals in the picture called?	The title of the picture is "Prairie Dog Home"	The animals in the picture are prairie dogs.
Where do these animals live?	The picture shows the animals in underground tunnels.	They live underground.
Why do these animals live underground?	It looks like bigger animals might try to hurt them.	They can be safe from bigger animals.

Good readers ask questions when they read because good questions lead to good answers! Questions help you pay closer attention to what you read. And they also help you get unstuck when you run into something confusing.

Read the first part of a science passage about beaver homes.

Genre: **Science**

Beaver Lodges   *By Bryan Davis*

Do you know the saying "busy as a beaver"? People say this because beavers are always working. These crafty creatures spend a lot of time building their homes.

Beaver homes are called lodges. They are found along streams, rivers, ponds, and lakes. Beavers build these homes from branches and rocks. They use mud to hold them together. When they can, beavers build their homes into the banks along the water. Other times, they first build a dam from logs, branches, and mud. They get the logs by gnawing at trees until they fall down. A dam is like a wall that blocks water. It then forms a pond. Once the dam is built, beavers can get to the business of building their lodge.

(continued)

Explore how to answer this question: *"What do beavers use to build their homes? Include details from the text in your answer."*

Underline details in the paragraphs above to find out what beavers use to build their homes.

Some details from the passage are shown in the chart below. Write another detail on the lines. Put quote marks around text taken from the passage.

Question	Details from Passage	Answer
What do beavers use to build their homes?	• "Beavers build these homes from branches and rocks." • _____ _____	Some things beavers use to build their homes are branches, _____.

Fill in the blank below to write about the answer you just found.

I found the answer to the question in paragraph number _____ of the passage.

Continue reading about beaver homes. Use the Close Reading and the Hint to help you answer the question.

Close Reading

Beavers have an interesting way of getting into their homes. Find and **underline** the sentence that tells why they have secret openings to their homes.

(continued from page 4)

Beaver lodges are shaped like a dome. They are usually about 10 feet high and 20 feet across. Most lodges have at least one underwater opening. To get inside, the beavers must swim underwater. These "secret" openings keep out unwanted predators.

Inside the beaver lodge are different "rooms." There is an eating room and a nesting room. The floor of the lodge is built up out of the water. It is also made from rocks, branches, and mud. It is covered with plants and other soft materials.

A family of beavers lives in a lodge. Two parents and two sets of their offspring often live together.

Hint

Which choice is a question that is answered by a detail in the passage?

Circle the correct answer.

Which question can be answered by reading the paragraphs above?

A   Where in the world can you find beavers?

B   How long does it take beavers to build a lodge?

C   Why do beaver lodges have underwater openings?

D   What do beavers like to eat?

✎ **Show Your Thinking**

Look at the answer that you chose above. Explain the answer to the question by using information in the passage.

_____

_____

 Pick one detail from an answer you did not choose. Tell your partner what information would need to be in the paragraph above to answer the question.

Read the science passage. Use the Study Buddy and Close Reading to guide your reading.

Genre: **Science**

After I read this passage, I'll write down some questions I have. For example, why do some animals like to turn termite mounds into their homes?

Termite Mounds *by Madeline Clark*

1   Some termites are called mound builders. They work together to build a nest from mounds of clay. Some of these mounds are more like towers. They stand almost 35 feet tall!

2   Mound builders are found in Africa, Australia, and parts of South America. Other animals in these areas also use termite mounds. Some wait until the termites move away. Others ignore the termites and use the mound anyway.

3   Termite mounds are usually the highest point on a plain. Cheetahs often climb to the top and use the mound as a lookout point. Cheetahs keep an eye out for their next meal from high atop the mound.

4   When the termites move on to a new nest, they leave their tall mounds behind. That's good news for animals that know how to put an empty termite mound to good use.

5   Some animals take over a termite mound and make it their home. Mongooses are small animals in Africa. They make a hole in the mound to get inside. The termite mound keeps them safe from other animals. Snakes also use an empty termite mound as a home.

6   Termite mounds also come in handy for large animals. Elephants and rhinos use them as scratching posts. Bug bites and dry mud can make any creature itchy. These large animals stand near a mound and rub against them. Sometimes they even stand over a mound to scratch their bellies!

Close Reading

What small animals use termite mounds? **Underline** the different animals mentioned in paragraph 5.

Why do some large animals like termite mounds? **Underline** a sentence that tells how large animals use them.

Hints

What do you find out about cheetahs in paragraph 3?

What animals does paragraph 5 describe? What do those animals do?

Reread paragraph 6. What do you learn about larger animals and termite mounds?

Use the Hints on this page to help you answer the questions.

1   Why do cheetahs like to climb up termite mounds?

   A   They can look far to see animals to hunt.

   B   They can sleep safely on top of termite mounds.

   C   They use termite mounds as scratching posts.

   D   They can call to each other more easily.

2   Which question can be answered by reading paragraph 5?

   A   How tall is a termite mound?

   B   Why do mongooses move into termite mounds?

   C   What large animals use termite mounds?

   D   What animals are mound builders?

3   Describe how rhinos and elephants use termite mounds. Use two details from the passage to support your answer.

_____

_____

_____

_____

_____

_____

_____

_____

_____

_____

_____

_____

Read the science article. Then answer the questions that follow.

Teeny Tiny Tardigrades

by Mary Reina, Highlights

1   What would you say if someone asked you to name Earth's toughest survivor? Camels can go a week without drinking. A cockroach can survive more radiation than a person. But there is a teeny tiny creature that can go without food or water for years. It is so small that it can be seen only under a microscope. Its real name is tardigrade. Most people call it a water bear.

Surviving Everything

2   Water bears look like soft, squishy bugs. People call them bears because they walk the way bears do. Most water bears are smaller than the period at the end of this sentence. Don't let their size fool you. They are found in places that would kill most living things.

3   Some water bears survive in the boiling water found in hot springs. Others live miles below the ocean surface. They survive with tons of water pressing down on them.

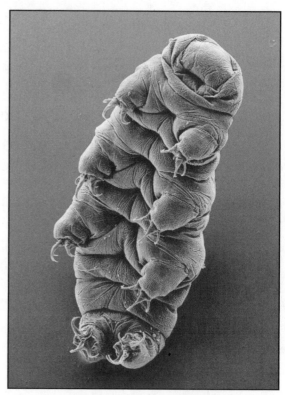

A tardigrade, photographed under a microscope

4   Not all water bears live in extreme places. They can be found in parks, forests, and gardens. They thrive in damp, woody areas where mosses and other plant life grow. Many feed by sucking juices out of plants. Others eat creatures that are smaller than they are.

Drying Up

5   Water bears must have water to stay active. It helps them eat, move, and breathe. So what happens when the water around one of these tiny creatures dries up? First, it pulls in its eight legs. Then, it curls its body into a barrel shape called a tun. It loses 99 percent of its water. Then every single life function of the water bear stops.

6   When conditions get better, the water bear stretches its little legs and starts moving and eating again.

7   Water bears can survive the extreme cold and radiation of outer space. Scientists sent some water bears into space as part of an unmanned mission. They came back fine!

8   Not so long ago, most scientists believed life did not exist beyond Earth. Now, many think it is possible. If water bears can survive a visit to outer space, who knows what other creatures might live there?

Answer the questions. Mark your answers to questions 1–3 on the Answer Form to the right.

Answer Form

1 Ⓐ Ⓑ Ⓒ Ⓓ
2 Ⓐ Ⓑ Ⓒ Ⓓ   **Number**
3 Ⓐ Ⓑ Ⓒ Ⓓ   **Correct** /3

1   Which question can be answered by reading paragraph 2?

  A How long can a camel go without water?

  B Why do people call tardigrades water bears?

  C Where do water bears live?

  D How do water bears eat?

2   Which sentence from the text shows what happens when a tardigrade doesn't have any water?

  A "Then every single life function of the water bear stops."

  B "They thrive in damp, woody areas where mosses and other plant life grow."

  C "When conditions get better, the water bear stretches its little legs and starts moving and eating again."

  D "But there is a teeny tiny creature that can go without food or water for years."

3   Read these sentences from the article.

  Water bears must have water to stay active. It helps them eat, move, and breathe.

Which question can be answered after reading these sentences?

A   How long can a water bear survive without water?

B   What food do water bears eat?

C   Where do water bears get their water?

D   Why is water important to water bears?

4   The article says that if alien life exists, it might be like tardigrades. Write a paragraph telling why this idea might be correct. Use **two** details from the article to support your answer.

_____

_____

_____

_____

_____

_____

_____

_____

 **Self Check**   *Go back and see what you can check off on the Self Check on page 1.*

Lesson 2   Part 1: Introduction 👥

Finding Main Ideas and Details

CCSS
RI.3.2: Determine the main idea of a text; recount the key details and explain how they support the main idea.

Theme: *World Communities*

The **main idea** of a passage is what the passage is mostly about. **Details** are all the facts and ideas in a passage. The most important **key details** in a passage support the main idea by giving more information about it.

Read the following passage about the way people lived in the American colonies.

> Life in the American colonies was not easy. People had to work very hard to make a living. Some families lived on farms and made their living by selling food to people in faraway towns. Getting to a town could take two hours or more. They had to travel by horse, which was not easy on the rough terrain. Once in town they sold their goods. Then they would take the long trip back to the farm.

Underline the first sentence of the passage. This is the main idea. Then circle three details that help explain why life in the American colonies was not easy.

The table below shows you how to keep track of a main idea and key details. Complete the table by filling in the last key detail.

Main Idea		
Life in the American colonies was not easy.		

Key Detail	Key Detail	Key Detail
People had to work hard to make a living.	Getting to town could take two hours.	_____ _____ _____

In the passage above, the first sentence told you the main idea. That doesn't always happen. Sometimes, the main idea doesn't show up until later in the passage. In this lesson, you will practice several ways to determine the main idea and key details.

Read the first part of a social studies passage about communities.

Genre: **Social Studies**

What Is a Community?   *by Clayton James*

A community is a group of people who live and work in the same area. People do different things to help make a community.

Think about the people you saw on your way to school today. Maybe you saw a bus driver. A bus driver helps get you to school on time and safely. Maybe you saw a police officer. A police officer makes sure that people follow the laws and stay safe. Maybe you saw a mail carrier, a delivery person, or people on their way to work. All of these people work together to make a community. This community is your city or town.

(continued)

Explore how to answer this question: *"What is a detail in the passage that supports the main idea?"*

First, look for a sentence that tells what the passage is mostly about. What is the main thing you learn from reading this passage?

The main idea and two details that support it are shown in the chart below. Find a third detail from the passage that supports the main idea by filling in the blank in the chart.

Main Idea
"A community is a group of people who live and work in the same area."

Key Detail	Key Detail	Key Detail
"A bus driver helps get you to school on time and safely."	"A police officer makes sure that people follow the laws and stay safe."	A city or town is a type of _____ .

Fill in the blank below to write about a detail that supports the main idea of the passage.

A detail that supports the main idea is that a city or town is a type of _____ .

Continue reading about communities. Use the Close Reading and the Hint to help you answer the question.

(continued from page 12)

Once you got to school, you saw teachers, other students, parents, and the principal. All of these people work together to help make your school community. They help make sure you have what you need to learn and be safe.

You are a part of your community, too. You do things to make a difference. You can help keep your community clean. You can follow rules and laws. You can help others in your community who are in need. You and everyone around you work together to make a community.

Close Reading

A paragraph also has a main idea. In the last paragraph, find and **underline** details that tell how you are part of your community.

Hint

Remember: The main idea isn't always the first sentence.

Circle the correct answer.

Which sentence best tells the main idea about what makes a town or city a type of community?

A "Once you got to school, you saw teachers, other students, parents, and the principal."

B "You are part of your community, too."

C "You can follow rules and laws."

D "You and everyone around you work together to make a community."

✏️ **Show Your Thinking**

Look at the answer that you chose above. Explain which details in the last paragraph support your answer.

_____

_____

 Pick one answer you didn't choose. Tell your partner why this answer is a detail, not a main idea.

Read this personal essay written by a Native American girl in the late 1800s. Use the Study Buddy and Close Reading to guide your reading.

Genre: **Personal Essay**

Life in My Village

by Maahe, a 19th-century Cheyenne Indian

The main idea isn't always stated in the first sentence of a passage. I'm going to reread the passage to see how the details add up to a main idea.

Close Reading

The essay tells what people do in the village. In paragraph 3, **circle** three activities that people do.

What is paragraph 4 mostly about? **Underline** a sentence in paragraph 4 that tells its main idea.

1   My name is Maahe. I am a Cheyenne Indian. I live with my family on the plains. We work hard in my village, but we also have fun. Each morning before the sun rises, people in my village build a fire. Then women walk to the stream to collect water. They use the water to make the morning meal.

2   After our morning meal, a man called the crier circles our village on a horse. He makes announcements. We all gather to hear the day's news.

3   After cleaning up from our morning meal, the children play games and swim. The women leave camp to gather sticks and roots. They tie the sticks into bundles and carry them back to camp on their backs.

4   We live in tipis made of buffalo hides. We can put them up or take them down quickly. The tipis are our homes. Because we follow the buffalo herds, we move often. We can pack up our entire village in one hour! Dogs or horses help pull all our belongings, including our tipis, on big sleds.

5   When we hunt buffalo, both men and women help. The women chase the buffalo toward the men. The men use their bows and arrows to kill the buffalo.

6   As evening falls, everyone gets ready for the evening meal. We eat, dance, tell stories, and play music. Then, everyone goes to sleep. We know tomorrow will be another busy day!

Hints

Pick the choice that describes the whole passage.

Choose a sentence that gives examples of what was mentioned in the main idea.

Reread paragraph 4. What details does the author give to help explain the main idea of this paragraph?

Use the Hints on this page to help you answer the questions.

1 What is one main idea of "Life in My Village"?

 A People in the village work hard but also have fun.

 B People in the village build a fire each morning.

 C Maahe and her family live in a village on the plains.

 D Women in the village make the morning meal.

2 Which sentence from the passage best supports the answer you chose for question 1 above?

 A "After our morning meal, a man called the crier circles our village on a horse."

 B "After cleaning up from our morning meal, the children play games and swim."

 C "We eat, dance, tell stories, and play music."

 D "When we hunt buffalo, both men and women help."

3 Explain why tipis are important to the people in Maahe's village. Use two details from paragraph 4 in your response.

_____

_____

_____

_____

_____

_____

_____

_____

_____

_____

Read the social studies passage. Then answer the questions that follow.

Living in the Clouds

by Jeanette Cannon

1   Imagine living in a place so high that clouds are everywhere. Not high in the sky, but all around! This is what life is like in the Andes. The Andes are very high mountains in South America. The Inca people have lived in the Andes Mountains in Peru for over 500 years. As you might guess, it is not easy making a living on high, rocky mountain land.

Mountain Farming

2   The mountainsides make for difficult farming in the Andes. Farmers cut giant steps into the mountain so they have a flat area to plant. They grow potatoes, corn, wheat, and grains. There are hundreds of different kinds of potatoes grown in the Andes. In other parts of the Andes, cotton, bananas, and sugarcane are grown.

3   The Incas raise sheep, llamas, guinea pigs, and alpacas. Llamas were important to the Inca people 500 years ago and still are today. They are used to carry heavy loads through the mountains. They are surefooted, which means they do not easily trip or fall. People drink llama's milk just as many other people drink cow's milk.

Made in Peru

4   Beautiful handmade objects come from Peru. Spinners and weavers especially like to work with the soft wool of llamas and alpacas. Spinners spin the wool into threads or yarn. People use the yarn to knit beautiful sweaters, scarves, and other cozy objects. Weavers form cloth from the threads to make blankets, handbags, and hats. Objects made in Peru are known for their bright colors.

Ancient Cities

5   Visitors come to Peru to see things they could not see anywhere else. One of the most famous places to visit is Machu Picchu. The Incas carved this city on a mountaintop. To get there, people can walk the same trail the Incas walked 500 years ago. It is important to keep the city and trail clean. Hikers and campers have to take their trash with them. Many people come every year. It is worth the trouble and sore legs to see the ruins of this beautiful Inca city.

Peru's Garden of Eden

6   Peru is home to Manu, one of the world's few rain forests. Many of the trees of the rain forest were being cut down. Some people are trying to stop that from happening. Rain forests are home to animals and plants that do not live anywhere else. Many travelers visit the rain forest. People who live there hope that will show how important it is to leave the rain forest alone.

7   Though life can be hard, the Inca people have found a way to make the most of what the land offers. And more and more visitors are learning a little about what life is like near the clouds.

Answer the questions. Mark your answers to questions 1–3 on the Answer Form to the right.

Answer Form

1 Ⓐ Ⓑ Ⓒ Ⓓ
2 Ⓐ Ⓑ Ⓒ Ⓓ   **Number** / 3
3 Ⓐ Ⓑ Ⓒ Ⓓ   **Correct**

---

1   Read this sentence from the passage.

> "Though life can be hard, the Inca people have found a way to make the most of what the land offers."

This sentence suggests that the Incas' way of life depends on what they can get from the land. Which sentence from the passage supports this idea?

A   "They grow potatoes, corn, wheat, and grains."

B   "Beautiful handmade objects come from Peru."

C   "One of the most famous places to visit is Machu Picchu. "

D   "Peru is home to Manu, one of the world's few rain forests."

2   Which sentence about llamas **best** explains the main idea of paragraph 3?

A   "The Incas raise sheep, llamas, guinea pigs, and alpacas."

B   "Llamas were important to the Inca people 500 years ago and still are today."

C   "They are surefooted, which means they do not easily trip or fall."

D   "People drink llama's milk just as many other people drink cow's milk."

3   How do the details about handmade objects help you understand the main idea of paragraph 4?

A   They describe which bright colors are used to make beautiful scarves and sweaters.

B   They describe how the Inca make different things from llama and alpaca wool.

C   They describe how sheep and llamas are used to make yarn for homemade objects.

D   They describe how blankets, handbags, and hats are made in factories.

4   Write a paragraph telling how the Incas in Peru live. Use **three** details from the text in your answer.

_____

_____

_____

_____

 **✓ Self Check**   *Go back and see what you can check off on the Self Check on page 1.*

Reading About Time and Sequence

CCSS

RI.3.3: Describe the relationship between a series of historical events, scientific ideas or concepts, or steps in technical procedures in a text using language that pertains to time, sequence....

Theme: *Westward Expansion*

Events in history are usually told in the order in which they happened, or in **time order**. Events can also happen in a **sequence**. Sequence shows how one thing leads to another, but not necessarily over time.

You can look for signal words that give clues about time order and sequence. *First, next,* and *finally* are signal words, as are *then, now, after, while,* and *when.*

Read the cartoon below.

First, in 1000 C.E., the Vikings got ready to sail across the ocean.

Then they sailed across the Atlantic Ocean.

Finally, the Vikings arrived in North America.

Now, read the cartoon again. This time, circle signal words that help you understand the order of events.

Now read the chart below to see how you can keep track of the order in which events happened. Write in the last event.

The Vikings Sail to North America		
First	**Next**	**Finally**
In 1000 C.E., the Vikings got ready to sail across the ocean.	They sailed across the Atlantic Ocean.	_____ _____

Good readers recognize the time order and sequence of events in a passage so they can keep track of when these events happened.

Read the first part of a history passage about the explorers Lewis and Clark.

Genre: **History**

Adventures of the Growing Nation   *by Teri Hillen*

Imagine that, in a single day, a country becomes twice as big as it was before. It might sound impossible, but that's what happened to the United States in 1803. The country doubled in size when the U.S. government persuaded the French to sell more than 828,000 square miles of land west of the Mississippi River.

President Thomas Jefferson asked Meriwether Lewis and William Clark to explore the mostly unknown area. To prepare, they first had a large boat built to take the men down the Ohio River. Then they built a base camp near St. Louis and spent the winter of 1803 there. Finally, on May 14, 1804, Lewis and Clark and about fifty men began their famous trip into the new territory.

(continued)

Explore how to answer this question: *"When did Lewis and Clark start on their journey? Look for this information in the text."*

This passage uses time dates to show the order of events. You'll need to match a date to the event to answer the question.

Look for dates and signal words in the passage to help you answer the question. Two events are shown in the chart below. Fill in the blank in the third box.

Lewis and Clark Expedition		
First	**Next**	**Finally**
Lewis and Clark built a large boat to take them down the Ohio River.	They spent the winter near St. Louis.	On _____ , Lewis and Clark began their exploration of the new area.

By placing events in time order, you can see when they happened.

Fill in the blank to tell when Lewis and Clark started their journey.

Lewis and Clark started their journey on _____ .

Continue reading about Lewis and Clark. Use the Close Reading and the Hint to help you answer the question.

Close Reading

Lewis and Clark came home to a big party in St. Louis. **Underline** the sentence that tells when the party was held.

(continued from page 20)

After traveling for almost 18 months, the group made it to the Pacific Ocean in November 1805. Clark wrote, "Ocean in view! O! The joy." The group spent a long, cold winter near the ocean. Then they began the trip back home in March 1806.

When Lewis and Clark arrived in St. Louis, Missouri, in September 1806, they were greeted with a big party. A century later, in 1904, the World's Fair was held in St. Louis. People honored Lewis and Clark's journey at the fair.

Hint

What year is almost 100 years after Lewis and Clark arrived back home in Missouri?

Circle the correct answer.

What happened almost 100 years after Lewis and Clark returned home?

A Their journey was honored at the World's Fair in St. Louis.

B They celebrated at a large party.

C They spent a cold winter near the ocean before heading home.

D Clark wrote about the joy of seeing the ocean.

✎ **Show Your Thinking**

Look at the answer that you chose above. Explain why this is the correct answer by telling the order of events in the paragraph.

_____

_____

_____

_____

 Pick one answer you didn't choose. To explain why it's not correct, tell your partner when the event in the answer happened.

Read the biography. Use the Study Buddy and Close Reading to guide your reading.

Genre: **Biography**

William Becknell and the Santa Fe Trail

by Joy Adams

This passage tells about events that happened long ago. I'm going to look for years and other dates to see when these events took place.

Close Reading

What happened in New Mexico while Becknell and his party were out on their first trip? **Underline** the sentence that tells what happened.

Paragraph 4 describes the second time Becknell traveled from Missouri to Santa Fe. **Circle** signal words that show the sequence of the route he took.

1   William Becknell was a trader and trapper. He was born in Virginia in the late 1700s. As a young man, Becknell moved to Missouri in 1810.

2   In Missouri, Becknell traded salt, but his business wasn't very successful. So, in the summer of 1821 he planned a trip West. Traveling on horseback, Becknell and his group hoped to trade horses and mules and trap animals.

3   When the party started their trip, Spain owned New Mexico. The Spanish didn't allow traders from the United States to sell their goods there. As the party made its way, however, the Spanish lost control. When Becknell's party learned this news, they headed straight to Santa Fe where they traded their goods for silver dollars.

4   About a year after returning from his first trip, in May 1822, Becknell and his wagons left Missouri once again. This time Becknell followed a dangerous route. First, he followed the Arkansas River to what is today Dodge City, Kansas. Then he traveled southwest to the Cimarron River. The party ran out of water and almost died. But Becknell pushed them on to the river. Finally, they reached Santa Fe. They had blazed a new trail!

5   Becknell's route became known as the Santa Fe Trail. In 1825 it was marked as the main route to the Southwest. This route was important to the expansion of the United States.

Hints

Look back at the dates you circled in paragraph 1. What happened in 1810?

Use the Hints on this page to help you answer the questions.

1 What did William Becknell do in 1810?

    A He trapped animals for their fur.

    B He began trading horses.

    C He traveled to Kansas.

    D He moved to Missouri.

What do you learn in paragraph 3 about New Mexico?

2 What happened during Becknell's first trip that made it possible for his party to trade in Santa Fe?

    A Becknell and his party found silver dollars.

    B The Spanish lost control of New Mexico.

    C Becknell and his party trapped many animals.

    D The Spanish opened New Mexico to the U.S.

Be careful. You need to find the *actual* order of events, not the order in which paragraph 4 tells each event.

3 The phrase box below lists four events that happened during Becknell's second trip to Santa Fe. The events are not in order.

Phrase Box	
ran out of water	reached the Cimarron River
arrived at Santa Fe	traveled to Dodge City

In the chart below, write the phrases from the phrase box in the order in which they happened to Becknell during his trip, from **earliest** to **latest**.

1.	2.	3.	4.

Read the biography. Then answer the questions that follow.

Sacajawea's Journey into History

by Jeanette Cannon

1   You may have seen this gold-colored dollar coin. It shows the face of a young Native American woman carrying a baby on her back. She is one of the only women on a U.S. legal coin. So who was she?

2   Sacajawea was a Shoshone Indian born at the end of the 1700s in an area now called Idaho. Her early life was difficult. Sometime between 1799 and 1801, she was captured by a group of Hidatsa Indians and taken away from her people. She was only 12 years old. By age 16, she was married to a French fur trader named Toussaint Charbonneau, who lived with the Hidatsas. Her adventures were just beginning.

3   In 1803, President Thomas Jefferson wanted to map out the newly expanded nation. He sent Meriwether Lewis and William Clark on an expedition to explore the land.

4   In 1804, the explorers began traveling on the Missouri River in canoes. One of their jobs was to take notes about what they saw. They drew pictures of plants and animals they saw. They made maps as they went along. They carried with them special tools to help them as they traveled. Everything was wrapped so water would not damage anything.

5   Many men had signed up to go on the expedition. One of them was Sacajawea's husband. In the spring of 1805, she and their new baby boy went along, too.

6   Though Sacajawea was not a guide on the journey, she helped the travelers in many ways. One of Lewis and Clark's diary entries from May 14, 1805 tells how Sacajawea's calm bravery saved important objects and information from being lost forever.

7   One day, a terrible storm caused Sacajawea's canoe to tip over. All the men were trying to get the canoe upright. Sacajawea calmly went into the water. Her baby was strapped to her back. She saved the notebooks and tools that would have floated away.

8   Later that year, the explorers came to Shoshone territory. Sacajawea helped them find a route through the mountains. She also helped them buy horses from her fellow Shoshone.

9   A few months later, the group had their first look at the Pacific Ocean. Before beginning the return journey, the explorers built a camp to stay in over the winter.

10   In May 1806, a few months after they had started their journey home, the travelers met a group of Nez Perce Indians. Sacajawea helped the two groups speak to each other. On the way back east, Sacajawea guided the group along trails she remembered from her childhood. One important trail was a gap in the mountains that led them to the Yellowstone River.

11   The journey ended for Sacajawea in August 1806. People who traveled with her wrote about her cheerfulness and helpfulness. They all said she showed great courage.

12   In 2000, two centuries after Sacajawea was born, a special U.S. dollar coin was created. It honors a brave young woman who helped explore a new nation.

Timeline of Some Events in the Life of Sacajawea

1788:	Sacajawea is born.
1799–1801:	Sacajawea is captured by Hidatsas.
Spring 1805:	Sacajawea, her baby, and her husband Charbonneau join the Lewis and Clark expedition.
May 14, 1805:	A sudden storm nearly capsizes one of the boats.
August 18, 1805:	Sacajawea helps Lewis and Clark trade for Shoshone horses.
December 7, 1805:	The explorers build Fort Clatsop and camp there for the winter.
May 11, 1806:	The group meets up with several Nez Perce chiefs. Charbonneau and Sacajawea translate.
July 15, 1806:	Sacajawea and the group reach Yellowstone River.
March, 1811:	Sacajawea and Charbonneau move to South Dakota.

Answer Form

1 Ⓐ Ⓑ Ⓒ Ⓓ
2 Ⓐ Ⓑ Ⓒ Ⓓ   **Number**
3 Ⓐ Ⓑ Ⓒ Ⓓ   **Correct** /3

1 What event happened **first** after Sacajawea helped the explorers buy horses from the Shoshone?

   A The group stayed at Fort Clatsop for the winter.

   B The group met with Nez Perce Indians.

   C Sacajawea married Toussaint Charbonneau.

   D Sacajawea helped the group find a route through the mountains.

2 According to the time line, which of the following events happened **first**?

   A Sacajawea signed up for an expedition with Lewis and Clark.

   B Sacajawea and the expedition reached Yellowstone River.

   C Sacajawea was captured by Hidatsas.

   D Sacajawea and Charbonneau moved to South Dakota.

3 What happened to Sacajawea that made her more likely to marry a fur trader?

   A She was taken away from her people at age 12.

   B She was born in Idaho in the late 1700s.

   C Her face was shown on a gold-colored dollar coin.

   D She was the first person to see the Pacific Ocean.

4 Write a paragraph telling why the United States honored Sacajawea with a coin. Use **two** events from the time line to support your answer.

_____

_____

_____

_____

✓ **Self Check** *Go back and see what you can check off on the Self Check on page 1.*

Lesson 4   Part 1: Introduction

Describing Cause and Effect

CCSS
RI.3.3: Describe the relationship between a series of historical events, scientific ideas or concepts, or steps in technical procedures in a text using language that pertains to . . . cause/effect.

Theme: *Weather and Climate*

When something causes another thing to happen, we say that the two events are connected by a cause and its effect. Understanding **cause** and **effect** helps us understand why things happen.

Writers often use words such as *because*, *if/then*, *since*, *therefore*, and *as a result* to describe and explain a cause and effect.

Look at the comic strip below. Think about what causes one thing to happen.

Henry got a balloon at the party.

Henry blew up the balloon.

The balloon popped because Henry blew it up too much!

Underline a signal word in the cartoon that helps you understand what caused the balloon to pop.

Now read the chart below to see how you can keep track of causes and effects when you read. Complete the chart by writing in the effect.

Cause (Why It Happened)	Effect (What Happened)
Henry blew up the balloon too much.	_____

Because Henry blew up the balloon too much, the balloon popped.

Good readers look for cause-and-effect connections to understand why things happen. Looking for signal words such as *because*, *since*, and *as a result* helps you spot cause-and-effect connections.

Read the first part of a science passage about clouds and rain.

Genre: **Science**

Cloudy with a Chance of Cats and Dogs

by Nicole Sheffler

You may have heard the saying, "It's raining cats and dogs out there!" But what's really going on up in the sky? Read on to find out how it all gets started.

Rain comes from clouds, but where do the clouds come from? First, it's important to understand that all air contains water. When warm air rises, the invisible water in it, called water vapor, starts to cool and expand. Since cold air can't hold all that water vapor, the vapor hitches a ride on tiny pieces of dust that are floating in the air. The vapor forms water droplets around the dust particles. A cloud is formed when billions of these water droplets come together.

(continued)

Explore how to answer this question: *"What causes water droplets to become a cloud?"*

Look for cause-and-effect connections in the passage that explain how clouds form.

Look at the chart below. Complete it by filling in the blank lines.

Cause	Effect
When warm air rises . . .	. . . the water vapor in the air cools and _____ .
Cold air can't hold too much water vapor, so . . .	. . . the vapor forms water droplets around _____ .
When many water droplets come together . . .	. . . they become a _____ .

When you read, pay attention to how and why things happen. This will help you understand cause and effect.

Fill in the blanks below to write about what causes water droplets to become a cloud.

Water droplets cause a cloud to form when _____ of them _____ together.

Continue reading about clouds and rain. Use the Close Reading and the Hint to help you answer the question.

Close Reading

Water droplets inside a cloud move and change. Find and **underline** the sentence that explains how they change.

(continued from page 28)

    Inside a cloud, the water droplets move around very quickly. As they move they may bump into each other. As a result, they may stick together. If they stick together, then they start to get bigger and bigger. When they get bigger, they get heavier. If they get too heavy for the cloud to hold them, they fall to the ground as rain. If it's cold outside, then they fall as snow.

    Much of this rain and snow falls all the way back down to the ground. Then the whole process starts over again.

Hint

Look for cause-and-effect words in the passage that tell about water droplets.

Circle the correct answer.

What causes water droplets in clouds to fall to the ground?

A They get really cold.

B They are warmed by the sun.

C They become heavy.

D They stop moving.

✎ Show Your Thinking

Look at the answer that you chose above. How is the correct cause of water droplets falling to the ground explained in more detail in the passage?

_____

_____

_____

 Pick one answer you didn't choose. Tell your partner why this answer does not explain why water droplets fall to the ground.

Read the science article. Use the Study Buddy and Close Reading to guide your reading.

Genre: **Science Article**

This article says that walruses' climate is getting warmer. I'll look for both the causes and the effects of this change to the climate.

Close Reading

The author says walruses must choose between food and rest. **Underline** a sentence that explains why they have to choose.

The article tells some effects of Arctic warming, but what are its causes? **Draw boxes** around two sentences that talk about possible causes.

More Ice Would Be Nice!

by Glenn Greenberg, Scholastic News

1   Walruses living near the frigid Arctic Circle are feeling the heat. The climate, or usual weather in a place, is getting warmer there. That means less sea ice. Without it, the walruses face a tough choice: food or rest!

2   Walruses rest and give birth on the sea ice. They feed their calves on these large frozen chunks. As the adults look for food, the calves stay on the ice. This helps to keep the calves safe from predators, or animals that live by hunting other animals for food.

3   In recent summers, however, the sea ice has melted faster. And in recent winters, less sea ice has formed because the weather was not cold enough.

4   Now, the sea ice in the Arctic is smaller and farther out in the sea—away from where the adult walruses look for food. That means they must swim longer to find food for themselves and their calves. The long swims make them very tired. It also means that their calves are left alone for longer periods of time, without protection or food.

5   Many scientists believe this climate change in the Arctic is part of a worldwide rise in temperature. This is called global warming. Some experts say it is happening naturally. Others believe it is caused by people burning fuel, such as when they drive cars or use a lot of electricity. . . .

Hints

Which choice shows that walruses must do something differently because of warming?

Use the Hints to help you answer the following questions.

1 How are walruses being affected by the warmer climate?

A They rest and give birth on sea ice.

B They must swim longer to find food.

C They leave their calves on the ice.

D They feed their calves on ice chunks.

Look at the sentence you underlined in the article. Does it match your answer to question 1?

2 Which sentence from the article best supports the correct answer to question 1 above?

A "This helps to keep the calves safe from predators, or animals that live by hunting other animals for food."

B "And in recent winters, less sea ice has formed because the weather was not cold enough."

C "Now, the sea ice in the Arctic is smaller and farther out in the sea—away from where the adult walruses look for food."

D "It also means that their calves are left alone for longer periods of time, without protection or food."

Which paragraph talks about why the Arctic is warming? Look back to find the details.

3 Explain what might be causing the Arctic to grow warmer. Use two details from the article to support your response.

_____

_____

_____

_____

_____

_____

_____

_____

_____

Read the science passage. Then answer the questions that follow.

How Hail Happens

by Val Dumitrescu

1   A soft rain is falling on the roof. It sounds nice. Suddenly, the sound gets louder. It sounds like golf balls are bouncing off the roof. You race to the window. Outside, round balls of ice cover the ground and bounce off the sidewalk. It is hailing! How does rain turn into hard hail in a matter of seconds?

Inside a Storm Cloud

2   It actually takes longer than a few seconds to form hail. It starts with a storm cloud. Storm clouds are made of water droplets. Large storm clouds are both very wide and very tall. The top of those clouds can reach high into the air. At the top, air is much colder than it is right above ground or even at the bottom of the cloud. Raindrops start to form at the bottom of the cloud, where it is warmer.

Journey of a Raindrop

3   As wind moves the storm cloud, it also moves some of the raindrops inside of it. Some of the raindrops move upward, to the top of the cloud. If the cold raindrops meet the very cold air at the top of the cloud, then they turn to ice. These new "ice drops," or hailstones, get heavier. As a result, they fall to the ground.

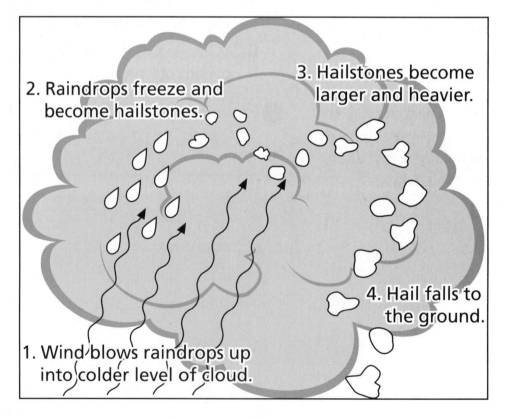

2. Raindrops freeze and become hailstones.

3. Hailstones become larger and heavier.

1. Wind blows raindrops up into colder level of cloud.

4. Hail falls to the ground.

Clear and Cloudy Hail

4   Some hail is very clear, like the ice cubes from your refrigerator. Other hail looks milky, like a piece of white chalk. When the hailstone is clear, it is because there is little air in it. That happens when the raindrops freeze slowly and the air bubbles in the water have time to escape. When the hailstone is milky looking, it is because the ice contains many small air bubbles. That happens when the air at the top of the cloud is super cold. That cold air turns the raindrops into ice almost immediately. The ice then traps the air bubbles.

Hailstones of Every Shape and Size

5   Sometimes, there are strong winds that move up through a cloud, instead of sideways. As a result, the wind can pick up the hailstones and send them back to the top of the clouds. At the top, the hailstones meet the cold air again and get a new coat of ice. In a strong thunderstorm, that can happen several times. When you look carefully at a hailstone, you may see some rings. Each ring is one layer of ice. If you count the rings then you'll be able to tell how many times the hailstone has made the trip to the top of the cloud. This up-and-down movement causes hailstones to have very unusual shapes. It also makes the hailstones bigger. Some hailstones can be the size of a pebble. Other hailstones can be larger than a baseball!

6   Next time you see hail gathering on your lawn, pick some up and look at it closely. It may have more of a story to tell than an ordinary ice cube.

Answer Form

1 Ⓐ Ⓑ Ⓒ Ⓓ
2 Ⓐ Ⓑ Ⓒ Ⓓ   **Number** ╱3
3 Ⓐ Ⓑ Ⓒ Ⓓ   **Correct**

1   The passage explains that wind causes raindrops to become hailstones by moving raindrops to the top of a cloud. Which sentence from the text **best** shows how the rain becomes hail?

A   "If the cold raindrops meet the very cold air at the top of the cloud, then they turn to ice."

B   "As wind moves the storm cloud, it also moves some of the raindrops inside of it."

C   "Raindrops start to form at the bottom of the cloud, where it is warmer."

D   "At the top, air is much colder than it is right above ground or even at the bottom of the cloud."

2   Why are some hailstones clear?

   A   Air bubbles get caught inside the hailstones.

   B   There is almost no air inside the hailstones.

   C   The temperature inside the cloud is very cold.

   D   There are strong winds inside the cloud.

3   What causes hailstones to have unusual shapes?

   A   Some hailstones break apart when they hit the ground.

   B   Super cold air inside a cloud breaks off parts of the hailstones.

   C   The hailstones get stuck in a storm cloud and never fall.

   D   The hailstones move up and down inside a cloud.

4   Write a paragraph telling what causes hailstones to get as big as baseballs.
Use **two** details from the passage to support your response.

_____

_____

_____

_____

_____

_____

_____

 **Self Check**   *Go back and see what you can check off on the Self Check on page 1.*

Read the history passage. Then answer the questions that follow.

A Race to the Rescue

by Lisa Torrey

1   In the winter of 1925, a deadly disease broke out in Nome, Alaska. The disease was a grave threat to the children who lived there. Only one kind of medicine could stop the disease from spreading. However, the medicine was in Anchorage, Alaska. Anchorage was nearly 1,000 miles away from Nome.

2   People were in a hurry to get the medicine from Anchorage to Nome. An old mail route linked the two towns. But the trip along the old route would be very hard. The route was covered with snow and ice. The howling winds were bitter cold. Rugged mountains also covered part of the route.

3   Their only hope was to rely on sled dogs. Sled dogs would be able to endure the long, cold journey and get the medicine quickly to Nome.

The Journey Begins

4   More than 20 mushers, or drivers, put together teams of sled dogs. Each team played a key part in the relay to race the medicine to Nome. The first team soon left Anchorage on the first leg of the trip.

5   Reporters wrote articles about the heroic race to deliver the medicine to Nome. People all around the world read these reports in newspapers. They followed each leg of the journey. They became caught up in the drama that was taking place in Alaska. They cheered for the dog sled teams, wanting them to succeed.

Balto Leads the Way

6   Amazingly, the team on the final stretch of the journey arrived in Nome only six days later. The musher drove his dog sled team into Nome on February 2, 1925. The team brought the medicine that would keep the children in Nome safe.

7   A husky named Balto was at the lead. Soon people all over the world saw pictures of Balto. People everywhere recognized his black furry face, pointed ears, and sparkling eyes. One year later, a group of people built a statue in honor of Balto. In 1926, they placed the statue in Central Park in New York City. Balto died in 1933.

8   Over four decades later, people in Alaska wanted to honor the heroic race that brought the medicine to Nome. They also wanted the race to celebrate the Alaskan frontier and the important role of sled dogs.

9   The Alaskans organized a sled dog race in 1967. It was a much shorter distance compared to the 1925 route. But in 1973, the first official Iditarod race was held. The race has been held every year since. The trail covers nearly 1,200 miles. Mushers and their teams of sled dogs come from all over to compete. It is called "The Last Great Race on Earth."

Statue of Balto in New York City

Answer Form

1	Ⓐ	Ⓑ	Ⓒ	Ⓓ	**Number**
3	Ⓐ	Ⓑ	Ⓒ	Ⓓ	**Correct**

 /2

1   Which sentence from the passage **best** supports the main idea of the passage?

    A   "A husky named Balto was at the lead."

    B   "The team brought the medicine that would keep the children in Nome safe."

    C   "They also wanted the race to celebrate the Alaskan frontier and the important role of sled dogs."

    D   "The first team soon left Anchorage on the first leg of the trip."

2   Paragraph 2 says the trip from Anchorage to Nome was "very hard." Explain why the trip was hard. Use **two** details from paragraph 2 to support your answer.

_____

_____

_____

_____

3   Which sentence from the passage shows why it was important to get medicine to Nome quickly?

     A   "The disease was a grave threat to the children who lived there."

     B   "People were in a hurry to get the medicine from Anchorage to Nome."

     C   "Each team played a key part in the relay to race the medicine to Nome."

     D   "Reporters wrote articles about the heroic race to deliver the medicine to Nome."

4   The phrase box below lists four events described in the passage. The events are not in order.

Phrase Box	
Balto's team brought medicine	first Iditarod race was held
statue of Balto was built	disease broke out in Alaska

In the chart below, write the events from the phrase box in the order in which they happened, from **first** to **last**.

First	Second	Third	Last

Read the science passage. Then answer the questions that follow.

Super Croc

By Susan Alexander

1   Imagine a time long ago when dinosaurs still walked the earth. It is a hot, sunny day. A young dinosaur steps into a river for a drink. He does not see the eyes watching him from the water. As he bends over to drink, huge jaws snap at him! He sees long rows of sharp teeth. He jumps back and runs away. He has just escaped a giant crocodile.

2   Crocodiles have been around for millions of years. The first ones lived at the time of the dinosaurs. Scientists have known that for a long time. But they didn't always know how huge some crocodiles were back then.

3   As big as crocodiles are today, they used to be even bigger. How big? Some were as long as school buses. And they were big enough to eat dinosaurs!

4   A few years ago, some scientists found bones in a desert in Africa. The desert was not always hot and dry. It once had many lakes and rivers. The bones belonged to a crocodile that had once lived there. That part did not surprise scientists. But they were surprised by how big the bones were. The bones belonged to the biggest crocodile anyone had ever known. They named the crocodile "Super Croc."

5   Even now, animals of all sizes need to watch out for crocodiles. They will eat anything they can catch. They often eat small animals like fish, turtles, and frogs. But some crocodiles grow very big and strong. They can catch animals three times their size. They will eat buffalo, hippos, and even lions!

6   There are 14 kinds of crocodiles living today. One is the Nile crocodile. It can grow up to 20 feet. It can weigh up to a ton, which is 2,000 pounds. That is one big animal! But it is nowhere near the size of Super Croc.

7   So just how big was Super Croc? It grew as long as 40 feet. That's twice as long as any living crocodile. Its head alone was six feet long. That is the size of a full-grown man. Super Croc weighed as much as ten tons. That's about as the same as four cars put together! And that's ten times as much as the biggest crocodiles today. In other words, Super Croc was super huge!

8   At the same time, Super Croc was like today's crocodiles in many ways. It may have lived to be 50 to 60 years old. That's about the same as crocodiles today. It ate fish and other animals. That's the same, too. It had babies by laying eggs that hatched.

9   You may be surprised to learn that crocodiles are good mothers. A mother may lay 20 to 80 eggs at once. After she hatches her eggs, she watches over the new babies. Mothers will stay with their young for a year.

10   Super Croc could walk around on land. But it was so big, it probably stayed in the water most of the time. The water supported its heavy body. That made it easier to move. It also made it easier to hunt. Super Croc could hide beneath the water. When other animals came to drink, Super Croc surprised them. It didn't matter much how big they were. To Super Croc, everything looked like dinner!

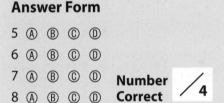

Answer Form

5 Ⓐ Ⓑ Ⓒ Ⓓ
6 Ⓐ Ⓑ Ⓒ Ⓓ
7 Ⓐ Ⓑ Ⓒ Ⓓ   **Number**
8 Ⓐ Ⓑ Ⓒ Ⓓ   **Correct** /4

5   What is the main idea of this passage?

     A   Crocodiles are much bigger today than they used to be.

     B   The biggest crocodile ever known lived millions of years ago.

     C   The Nile crocodile is nearly the same size as Super Croc was.

     D   Scientists found old crocodile bones in a desert in Africa.

6   According to information in paragraph 4, why were scientists surprised when they found crocodile bones in Africa?

     A   They were surprised to find the bones in a desert.

     B   They did not know that crocodiles lived in Africa.

     C   They were surprised by the large size of the crocodile bones.

     D   They did not know that crocodiles lived at the time of the dinosaurs.

7   Which question can be answered by reading paragraph 5?

    A   Where do crocodiles sleep?

    B   How big were Super Crocs?

    C   What do crocodiles eat?

    D   Where do crocodiles live?

8   How are today's crocodiles different from Super Croc?

    A   Today's crocodiles will eat anything they can catch.

    B   Today's crocodile can grow up to 20 feet.

    C   Today's crocodiles hunt large animals.

    D   Today's crocodiles live to be 50 to 60 years old.

9   The author shows that crocodiles are good mothers. Write a paragraph telling how crocodiles are good mothers. Use **three** details from the passage to support your answer.

_____

_____

_____

_____

_____

_____

Performance Task—Extended Response

10 Super Croc was much, much bigger than today's crocs! But just like Super Croc, today's crocs live to be about 50 to 60 years old. How else was Super Croc like crocodiles today? Tell **two** ways. Be sure to include details from the passage in your answer.

In your answer, be sure to
• tell **two** ways that Super Croc and today's crocs are alike
• use details from the passage in your answer

Check your writing for correct spelling, grammar, capitalization, and punctuation.

Use the space below to plan your essay.

Write your essay on the lines below.

_____

_____

_____

_____

_____

_____

_____

_____

_____

_____

_____

_____

_____

_____

Unit 2
Key Ideas and Details in Literature

You probably have heard the story "Jack and the Beanstalk." What is the first thing you remember about it? Most likely it's Jack and the giant. These are two of the characters. What do you remember about Jack's adventures? Is it how Jack climbs up the beanstalk? Or is it the part about Jack escaping from the giant? These are some of the important events in the story. Do you remember enough of the story to tell it in your own words? Perhaps you remember that it ends "happily ever after!" What do you like best about "Jack and the Beanstalk"? Have you read other stories that remind you of this story?

In this unit, you will learn to ask and answer questions about stories like "Jack and the Beanstalk." You will think about what characters say and do, and why. You'll pay attention to story events and see how one event leads to another. And you'll put all this together to figure out the message, or lesson, of the story. So get ready for a journey into storyland!

✓ Self Check

Before starting this unit, check off the skills you know below. As you complete each lesson, see how many more you can check off!

I know how to:	Before this unit	After this unit
ask and answer different kinds of questions about a story.	☐	☐
tell how and why characters make one event lead to another in stories.	☐	☐
tell the most important parts of a story using my own words, and in the order they happen.	☐	☐
describe the lesson that the characters learn in a story.	☐	☐

Lesson 5   Part 1: Introduction 👥

Asking Questions About Stories

CCSS

RL.3.1: Ask and answer questions to demonstrate understanding of a text, referring explicitly to the text as the basis for the answers.

Theme: *Discoveries*

It's important to keep track of what's going on in a story by asking questions as you read. The answers to some questions can be found in one sentence of the story. Think of them as "right-there" questions. To answer other questions, you may need to think about and search for details in different parts of the story. Think of these as "think-and-search" questions. Let's practice this. Read the following paragraph.

> Erika was doing her homework. Her pencil rolled off the desk and under the bed. She was under the bed looking for it when she saw an old wooden box she had never seen before. *How did that get there?* she asked herself. When Erika opened it, she saw gold coins glittering in the dim light. "Wow!" she said, "I think it's a treasure chest."

Write a question that could be answered by details in this paragraph. Underline the parts of the paragraph where you can find your answer.

_____

_____

Look at the chart to see how a "right-there" question and a "think-and-search" question can be answered by looking at story details.

Question	Story Details	Answer
Right-There Question: What does Erika find under the bed?	"She was under the bed looking for it when she saw an old wooden box she had never seen before."	Erika finds an old wooden box under her bed that she has never seen before.
Think-and-Search Question: Why does Erika think she has found a treasure chest?	"When Erika opened it, she saw gold coins glittering in the dim light."	Erika thinks she has found a treasure chest because treasure chests in stories are often filled with gold coins.

Good readers ask questions about what's happening in a story and whom it's happening to. They also ask questions about where and why the events happen.

Read the first part of a story about a girl and her grandmother.

Genre: **Realistic Fiction**

Grandma's Secret   *by Kat Williams*

Annie dreamed of being a famous singer. She and her grandmother both liked watching TV shows that made real people into singing stars.

One night Grandma brought down a box from the attic. "I'd like to show you some old photographs," she said. "I think you might find them interesting."

One photo showed four girls singing on a stage. Their hair was done up, and they wore matching dresses. "Who are those people?" Annie asked.

"That's me on the right," Grandma said. Annie looked closely.

"I see you! What are you doing?"

"I'm singing on a TV show with my group, The Wildflowers," Grandma said.

(continued)

Explore how to answer this question: *"What is shown in the photograph that Annie looks at with Grandma?"*

What kind of question is this? It's a "think-and-search" question. To find the answer, you need to look at several details in the story and put them together.

Look for story details that help you identify what is in the photo. Two details are provided for you below. Write one more detail on the lines. Then fill in the blanks in the Answer column.

Story Details	Answer

• "One photo showed four girls singing on a stage."
• "That's me on the right," Grandma said.
 	
• _____
  _____
  _____
	The photo shows Grandma
	
	_____
	
	with her group,
	
	The _____.

The details that answer the question are in three different sentences. By putting these details together, you can answer the question about what the photo shows.

Continue reading about Annie and her grandmother. Use the Close Reading and the Hint to help you answer the question.

Close Reading

What does Grandma tell Annie about the song she sang on TV? **Underline** sentences that tell how she came to sing on TV.

(continued from page 46)

"It was 40 years ago," Grandma said. "We recorded a song, and it played on the radio. It was so popular that we were asked to sing it on TV."

"Why didn't you tell me this before?" asked Annie.

Grandma smiled. "Oh, I guess I haven't thought about it for a long time."

Now it was Annie's turn to smile. "So, Grandma, what else have you done that you haven't told me about?"

Hint

Why were The Wildflowers asked to sing on TV?

Circle the correct answer.

Why did Grandma sing a song on TV?

A   The Wildflowers asked her to sing with them.

B   Her group had a popular song on the radio.

C   She won a contest on a TV show.

D   She heard about the TV show on the radio.

✎ **Show Your Thinking**

Pick one of the answers you did not choose. Tell why you think it does not answer the question correctly.

_____

_____

_____

 Think of another question that can be answered by reading the story. Ask your partner the question. Then discuss which details from the story help answer the question.

Read the story. Use the Study Buddy and the Close Reading to guide your reading.

I'm going to write down my questions when I reread this story. For example, I wonder how Everest keeps from falling when he steps off the cliff.

Close Reading

How does Everest learn to climb? **Underline** two sentences that tell about learning the basics of climbing.

How does Everest feel when he first tries to step backward off the cliff? **Draw a box** around the paragraph that tells what happens to him.

Genre: **Realistic Fiction**

from "A Boy Called Everest"

by Jennifer R. Hubbard, Cricket

1   I was forbidden to climb rocks. Rock climbing was the first step, and my mother knew it. My father's friends could've taught me what I needed to know, but she wouldn't allow it.

2   She didn't know that I went anyway. I taught myself the basics on boulders and small rockfaces, learned about handholds and toeholds and balance. By the time I was fifteen, I was climbing regularly. I bought gear and hid it from her, keeping some of it at my friend Scott's house.

3   My father named me Everest. People are always asking if I'm named after the mountain. "That's right," I tell them.

4   My friend Scott's father knew that my dad had been a big-time mountaineer, so he believed me when I said I had permission to climb. He taught Scott and me the basics, like how to rappel.

5   When that first moment came for me to step backward off the cliff's edge, I couldn't do it. I had the harness on, and my brain knew I wouldn't fall, but my body refused to step down into nothing. Scott snickered.

6   "Wait till it's your turn," I told him.

7   His father gave me a pep talk, which I didn't even hear. I thought of Everest, almost six miles high. I thought of the Yellow Band and the Hillary Step and all the other places I was never going to see if I didn't just move my foot. So I stepped backward off the cliff and I didn't fall.

Hints

Which sentence in paragraph 2 helps you answer this question?

1 Describe how Everest keeps his climbing a secret from his mother. Use two details from the story in your answer.

_____

_____

_____

_____

_____

_____

Which sentence in paragraph 4 gives you the answer to this question?

2 Who teaches Everest and Scott the basics of mountain climbing, such as how to rappel?

   A Everest's father

   B Scott's father

   C Everest's father's friends

   D Everest's mother

Look back at the paragraph you boxed to see the first thing Scott does when it is his turn.

3 Which sentence from the story tells what happens to Everest when it's time for him to take a step off the cliff?

   A "My friend Scott's father knew that my dad had been a big-time mountaineer, so he believed me when I said I had permission to climb."

   B "So I stepped backward off the cliff and I didn't fall."

   C "I had the harness on, and my brain knew I wouldn't fall, but my body refused to step down into nothing."

   D "His father gave me a pep talk, which I didn't even hear."

Read the story. Then answer the questions that follow.

An Earful

by Dale-Marie Bryan, Highlights

1   "Your homework is to collect sounds," Mrs. Olson said. She handed out sheets of paper shaped like giant ears. Then she held up a shiny blue kazoo. "Everyone who gets an 'earful' will get one of these." The class laughed.

2   Later, Jacob glared out the schoolbus window. Not fair, he thought. How could he collect enough sounds on his family's farm? There were plenty of noises in town. If only he lived where tires squeal.

3   Jacob scrambled off the bus when it screeched to a stop at his mailbox. But he wasn't in the mood to wave as it drove away.

4   When he threw open the gate, it groaned like a ghost. That was how he felt about his homework.

5   On the porch, Jacob knelt beside the kittens curled on the rug. They sounded like tiny motors when they purred.

6   "I'm home!" Jacob called. He thumped his book bag down on a kitchen chair.

7   The rocker in the nursery stopped creaking.

8   "How was school?" his mother asked, walking in with his baby brother on her shoulder. She was patting his little back.

9   "I've got homework," Jacob grumbled.

10   The baby burped, and Jacob laughed. "That's what I think about it, too!"

11   "Have a snack before you do your chores," his mother said. She took the animal crackers down from the cupboard.

12   Jacob rattled the carton. Not many left. He crunched two tigers, three lions, and a seal, then gulped down some milk. Grrr, roar, ork! If only animal crackers were real. He would have plenty of noises to list!

13　　Goldie, Jacob's collie, woofed as Jacob walked toward the barn. Her puppies were yipping in a straw-filled stall. Jacob plinked dog-food pellets into their pan, and the pups snuffled and crunched.

14　　In the chicken house, Jacob shooed two cackling hens from their nests. He slipped their warm eggs into his jacket. Wouldn't it be funny if he forgot about the eggs and they hatched? He'd have a peeping pocket!

15　　In the corral, a black cow napped in the sun. Jacob woke her when he poured corn into her pan. "Moo, thank you!" she seemed to say.

16　　Tap, clatter, clink. Dad drove the tractor into the yard. The lid on the tractor's smokestack rattled when it chuffed and chugged to a stop.

17　　"How was school?" Dad asked, stepping down from the cab.

18　　Jacob shrugged. "OK, I guess," he said. "I have some homework."

19　　Jacob put the eggs in the kitchen, then climbed to his tree house. He could see Dad's beehives by the hay field. Six hives usually meant plenty of humming. But today he couldn't hear it over the scolding of the blue jays and the chattering of the sparrows. How could a person think?

20　　"QUIET!" Jacob shouted.

21　　Suddenly, he sat up straight. Cows mooed and puppies yipped. Chickens cackled in their yard. When Goldie began barking below, Jacob grinned. There were plenty of noises on the farm. "I hear you!" he called. He hurried down from the tree. He had an earful of homework to do.

1　　What is Jacob's mother doing when Jacob comes home from school?

Answer Form

1 Ⓐ Ⓑ Ⓒ Ⓓ
2 Ⓐ Ⓑ Ⓒ Ⓓ　　**Number**　／3
4 Ⓐ Ⓑ Ⓒ Ⓓ　　**Correct**

　　A　taking care of Jacob's baby brother

　　B　fixing Jacob a snack in the kitchen

　　C　sitting on the porch with the kittens

　　D　feeding animals in the barn

2 Which sentence from the story tells why Jacob is upset about his homework assignment?

   A "Everyone who gets an 'earful' will get one of these."

   B "How could he collect enough sounds on his family's farm?"

   C "There were plenty of noises in town."

   D "Later, Jacob glared out the schoolbus window."

3 Write a paragraph telling why Jacob wishes the animal crackers were real. Use **two** details from the story to support your answer.

_____

_____

_____

_____

_____

4 Where is Jacob when he understands how many sounds there are to hear on the farm?

   A near the beehives

   B in the chicken house

   C in the corral

   D in his tree house

 **Self Check** *Go back and see what you can check off on the Self Check on page 43.*

Describing Characters

CCSS

RL.3.3: Describe characters in a story (e.g., their traits, motivations, or feelings) and explain how their actions contribute to the sequence of events.

Theme: *Curious Characters*

Characters are the people or animals in a story. When you read a story, think about what the characters say and do, and why. Just like real people, characters have feelings. They also have **traits,** or special qualities, such as courage, pride, cheerfulness, or honesty.

Following the **sequence,** or the order of events, in a story can help you understand how the characters' actions make one event lead to another.

Circle the parts of the cartoon that help you understand more about the giant, such as how this character feels, what he is like, and why he does what he does.

Now look at the chart below to see how details can help you understand what a character is like and how a character's words and actions lead the story forward.

What the Giant Does	What the Giant Says	What the Giant Is Like	How the Giant Moves the Story Forward
• He smiles. • He lifts the climbers over the mountain.	"I'll be here when you want to go home."	The giant is friendly and helpful.	Because the giant is friendly, he helps the climbers get over the mountain.

Good readers use details from the story to understand the reasons that characters act and speak as they do. They can use this information to figure out how the characters' actions contribute to the sequence of events.

Read the first part of a story about a real person named Susan B. Anthony.

Genre: **Historical Fiction**

Voting for Her Rights   *by Winnie Lujack*

In 1872, Susan B. Anthony did something dangerous. She told a group of women they should vote. At that time, only men had the right to vote.

"We're sure to get in big trouble," someone said.

"I know," Anthony said. "We should expect to be arrested and put on trial. But don't you see, we have to do it? How else will we show how much we want our voting rights?"

Two weeks after Election Day, a man knocked on Anthony's door.

(continued)

Explore how to answer this question: *"Why isn't Susan B. Anthony afraid of getting in trouble? Use details from the story in your answer."*

Think about how Susan B. Anthony feels about voting rights for women. What is she willing to do to win these rights?

Look for details that show what Susan B. Anthony is like and how what she says and does moves the story forward. Fill in the blanks in the chart.

What Susan Does	What Susan Says	What Susan Is Like
In 1872, she tells a group of women to _____ .	"We should expect to be _____ and put on trial. But don't you see, we have to do it? How else will we show how much we want our _____ _____ ?"	She feels strongly that women should have the right to _____ .

Fill in the blanks below to explain why Susan B. Anthony isn't afraid of getting in trouble.

She is willing to get _____ and put on _____ to show how much

she believes women should have the _____ .

Continue reading about Susan B. Anthony. Use the Close Reading and the Hint to help you answer the question.

Close Reading

Susan wanted others to think her beliefs were good. **Underline** sentences that tell why she thought fighting for rights was good.

(continued from page 54)

The man at the door was a police officer. He arrested Susan for voting when she didn't have a legal right to do it.

Before her trial, Susan traveled all around the United States to remind people how Americans had fought for their rights. She said that those rights belonged to women, too.

Susan was found guilty of voting. The judge told her that she would have to pay a fine as punishment. Although she lived for 33 more years, she never paid that fine.

Hint

How did Susan feel about being punished for voting?

Circle the correct answer.

Which words best describe Susan B. Anthony?

A frightened and weak

B carefree and happy

C brave and strong

D silly and careless

Show Your Thinking

Write two details from the story that show why the answer you chose is correct.

_____

_____

_____

_____

 What is your opinion about Susan B. Anthony never paying her fine for voting? Use details from the story to discuss your opinion with your partner.

Read the myth. Use the Study Buddy and the Close Reading to guide your reading.

Genre: **Myth**

Hmm. Pandora and Epi seem very different. I'm going to reread the story and find places that show how what they do and say moves the story forward.

Close Reading

What does Epi do that makes Pandora upset? **Underline** a sentence that tells what he does.

What kind of a person is Pandora? **Circle** one thing she says that shows what she is like.

Here Comes Trouble   *from a Greek myth*

1   Long ago, Pandora and her brother Epi were playing outside when something strange fell out of the sky and landed at Epi's feet. It was a small box that glowed green and purple! Epi eagerly bent down to pick it up, but Pandora held him back.

2   "Be careful," she warned. "I had a dream about a box like this one. In the dream, an old man warned me not to open it."

3   "Aw, come on, Pandora," Epi pleaded. "How much danger could there be in one little box? Besides, I bet there's treasure inside. I want to find out!"

4   "It's better to be safe than sorry," Pandora warned. "Let's go home right now—and leave the box behind."

5   But as soon as Pandora turned to leave, Epi quickly opened the box. Suddenly, the sky was filled with little stinging creatures. He slammed the box shut and started swatting at them. Pandora swung around in horror.

6   "Oh, Epi, what have you done?" she cried out. After a short time, however, the little creatures flew off in all directions. Only then did Epi and Pandora hear a little voice coming from the closed box.

7   "Don't be afraid," the voice whispered. "I'm here to help you."

8   Pandora thought carefully for a moment. Then she slowly opened the box. A tiny green and purple fairy flew out.

9   "I am Hope," the fairy said. "You let all the troubles of the world out of this box, but I was put in the box to comfort the world. I will be with you always."

10   Epi felt sad that he hadn't listened to his sister. "Don't worry, Epi," she said kindly. "At least we have Hope."

Hints

Reread paragraph 3. How does Epi feel about the box?

Use the Hints on this page to help you answer the questions.

1 At the beginning of the story, why does Epi want to open the box?

A He is curious to find out if the box is filled with treasure.

B He believes that the warning in Pandora's dream is only for her.

C He doesn't care if something bad happens when he opens the box.

D He knows that a green and purple fairy lives in the box.

What does the fairy tell Epi and Pandora about the creatures?

2 How do Epi's actions change the world?

A By slamming the box shut, he keeps most of the troubles inside.

B By opening the box, he brings Hope to the world.

C By opening the box, he lets out all the troubles of the world.

D By slamming the box shut, he traps Hope inside forever.

Look for clues about a character in what she says or does. Does Pandora say anything cautious?

3 The author shows that Pandora is a cautious person. Write a paragraph telling how Pandora is cautious. Use two details from the story to support your answer.

_____

_____

_____

_____

_____

_____

_____

Read the story. Then answer the questions that follow.

Cleopatra Finds Her Voice

by Vicki Alvear Shecter, Highlights

1   Eleven-year-old Princess Cleopatra sailed the Nile River on the royal barge. Her father, the king of Egypt, played his flute.

2   They were sailing from their palace in Alexandria to cities along the Nile. The king would often lead important ceremonies.

3   Cleopatra watched for slithering crocodiles and yawning hippos. Sometimes she would catch a glimpse of a Sacred Ibis bird tiptoeing along the marshy banks.

4   As the royal barge sailed, people crowded the banks, hoping to see the princess and her father. They sang and chanted and threw flowers. But it bothered Cleopatra that she could not understand what they said.

5   Her father explained that the people of Egypt spoke Egyptian, while Cleopatra's family spoke Greek.

6   But her father was the ruler of Egypt! Why didn't he and his family speak the native language?

7   They could thank their ancestors for that, the king said. The royal family traced its history back 250 years to the time of the Greek conqueror Alexander the Great. Alexander had conquered Egypt. When he died, his Greek general, Ptolemy, took over. Ever since, all of the rulers of Egypt had spoken Greek.

8   Once back at home, Cleopatra insisted on learning the Egyptian language. She believed that a ruler should know her people. And that meant knowing their words.

9   Cleopatra studied hard and soon learned to speak Egyptian. But she didn't stop there. She also learned Hebrew, Aramaic, Persian, Latin, and some African dialects. She loved learning and excelled in math and science, too.

10   Later, when she ruled as queen, one of her first acts was to visit the city of Memphis for an important religious ceremony. This time, she spoke to the people in Egyptian. The people loved her for learning their language. She showed them respect and honor in many other ways, too.

11   Cleopatra is remembered as a brilliant queen. She was the only Egyptian ruler in hundreds of years to learn the language of her people.

Ancient Egyptian Picture Writing
Known as Hieroglyphs

Answer the questions. Mark your answers to questions 1–4 on the Answer Form to the right.

Answer Form

1 Ⓐ Ⓑ Ⓒ Ⓓ
2 Ⓐ Ⓑ Ⓒ Ⓓ
3 Ⓐ Ⓑ Ⓒ Ⓓ   **Number**   /4
4 Ⓐ Ⓑ Ⓒ Ⓓ   **Correct**

1   What best explains why Cleopatra wants to learn to speak Egyptian?

A   She hopes it will help her with her studies of math and science.

B   She sees the love the people show for her father and for her.

C   Her father explains the history of her family's language.

D   She believes that as a ruler of Egypt, she should know Egyptian.

2   Which is the **most likely** reason that Cleopatra's father doesn't speak Egyptian?

A   Rulers of Egypt had spoken Greek for 250 years.

B   Alexander the Great had banned the teaching of Egyptian.

C   The king is more interested in playing the flute than learning a new language.

D   Cleopatra's father and the Greek general Ptolemy had agreed not to speak Egyptian.

3 What does Cleopatra find out about herself after she learns to speak Egyptian?

   A Speaking Egyptian helps her understand her religion better.

   B She no longer thinks her father is a good king.

   C Her family's old language no longer sounds right.

   D She has a love for learning for many languages.

4 Which sentence from the story tells that Cleopatra was a caring person?

   A "As the royal barge sailed, people crowded the banks, hoping to see the princess and her father."

   B "She believed that a ruler should know her people."

   C "She loved learning and excelled in math and science, too."

   D "Cleopatra is remembered as a brilliant queen."

5 The author shows that Cleopatra was a curious person. Write a paragraph telling how Cleopatra was curious. Use **two** details from the story to support your response.

_____

_____

_____

_____

_____

_____

 ✓ **Self Check** *Go back and see what you can check off on the Self Check on page 43.*

Lesson 7 **Part 1: Introduction**

Recounting Stories

CCSS

RL.3.2: Recount stories, including fables, folktales, and myths from diverse cultures.

Theme: *Stories from Around the World*

Recounting a story means telling the details of the story in the order they happen and in your own words. You don't need to recount every detail, but be sure to recount the important ones. The important ones are those that tell *who, what, where, when,* and *why.*

Read the story below. For now, just get a sense of what happens in it.

A Bundle of Sticks

Long ago, a mother had three children who were always arguing. "Your arguing sounds worse than the clucking of all the hens in the world," their mother told them. She wanted them to stop!

One day she got an idea. She gathered the children around her. Then she took a stick and broke it. "See how easy it is to break one stick?" she asked. Then she tied three sticks together. She asked each child to try to break the sticks. None of the children could break the bundle.

The mother told the children, "We're just like the sticks. When we don't stay together, our family is weak. When we stay together, nothing can break us apart."

The children understood! From that day forward, they didn't argue (as much).

Now read the story again. This time, as you read, underline three important details.

Did the details you underlined tell *who, what, where, when,* or *why*? Those are the important details to include when you recount a story.

Now look at the chart below. It shows how to organize the most important details of a story in the order they happen.

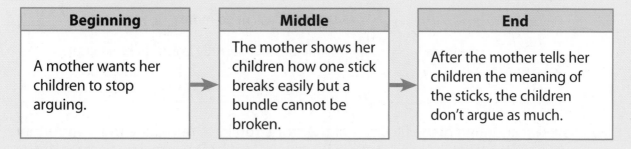

Beginning	Middle	End
A mother wants her children to stop arguing.	The mother shows her children how one stick breaks easily but a bundle cannot be broken.	After the mother tells her children the meaning of the sticks, the children don't argue as much.

When you recount a story, first find the most important details. Then put them together in order and tell them in your own words.

Read the first part of a folktale about a brother and sister trying to help each other.

Genre: **Folktale**

Brother and Sister   *a folktale from Korea*

Long ago, a brother and sister grew rice to sell. Through the long summer, they worked together to care for the rice paddies. In the fall, they harvested all the rice and put the rice into bags. Each got the same number of bags.

After one harvest, the brother announced he was soon to be married. The sister knew her brother would need money to buy a new house for his bride. She didn't feel the rice was divided fairly, so that night, she took an extra bag of rice to her brother's house in secret.

The brother, too, felt the rice was not divided fairly. His sister had a large family. She would need more rice. So that night, the brother took an extra bag to his sister's house in secret.

(continued)

Explore how to answer this question: *"What details should be in a recounting of this story?"*

To recount a story, first look for the most important details in each paragraph.

Fill in the blanks in the chart below to recount the most important details in the beginning and the middle of the story.

Beginning	Middle
A brother and sister grow and sell rice. They each get the same number of _____ .	• The brother will need _____, so the sister secretly brings him an extra _____. • The sister will need more _____, so the brother secretly brings her an extra _____.

Now you have a recounting of the first part of the story. You have retold the most important details in the order they happen. Remember to use your own words when recounting a story.

Close Reading

Underline the detail that tells why the brother and sister think something is strange. **Circle** the detail that solves the mystery.

Hint

Tell about the most important parts of the story. Use the chart on page 62 to help you with the beginning and middle parts.

Read the end of "Brother and Sister." Use the Close Reading and the Hint to help you complete the activity that follows.

(continued from page 62)

The next day, the brother and sister counted their rice bags. Strange! Both had the same number as before. So that night, when the moon was full, they made another attempt. In the moonlight, the brother and sister each saw the other carrying a bag of rice! They laughed. The mystery was solved.

Read the sentences below. Then write your response on the lines.

Reread all of "Brother and Sister." Then recount it on the lines below. Use the sentences you wrote in the chart to begin your recounting.

_____

_____

_____

_____

_____

_____

_____

_____

✎ **Show Your Thinking**

🗨 Read your recounting to your partner. Then listen to your partner's recounting. Discuss how your recountings of the story are alike and different.

Read the folktale. Use the Study Buddy and the Close Reading to guide your reading.

When I recount a story, what parts do I need to tell? I'll write one sentence about the beginning, another about the middle, and a third about the ending. Then I'll put them together in the right order.

Close Reading

How does the bat fly? **Circle** words that describe how she flies.

What are the most important events in the story? **Underline** the most important events and order them by placing a number in front of each.

Genre: **Folktale**

How the Bat Got Wings   *a Cherokee Nation tale*

1   A long time ago, the bat was a tiny mammal. It had no wings. One day, the mammals and birds decided to play a game. The birds played on one team, and the mammals played on the other team.

2   The bat wanted to play with the mammals, but the mammals laughed at her size. "You are too small," they said.

3   So the bat asked to play with the birds. The birds said, "You don't have wings, but we can make you some out of a drum." The birds stretched the skin of a drum into wings.

4   The birds put the wings on the bat and said, "Flap your wings." When the bat jumped off a tree and flapped her wings, she didn't fly in a straight line like the birds. Instead, she flew every which way in a crazy, zigzag pattern.

5   The birds let the bat play on their team, and just as she had done before, the bat flew in a crazy, zigzag pattern. The mammals on the other team could not catch the bat. The bat scored the winning points for the birds.

6   When the game was over, the mammals said, "Who is that superstar on your team?"

7   The birds said, "It is the bat. We gave her wings."

8   The mammals did not know what to say, for they had refused to let the tiny bat play on their team. However, they learned their lesson, and from that day on, they let any animal of any size play on their team.

Hints

How do the birds make it possible for the bat to play in the game?

Use the Hints on this page to help you answer the questions.

1 The chart below shows the order of some events in the story.

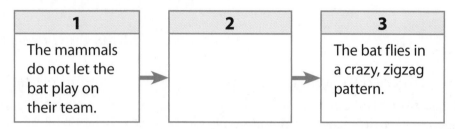

1	2	3
The mammals do not let the bat play on their team.		The bat flies in a crazy, zigzag pattern.

Which of the following sentences belongs in the empty box?

A Mammals and birds decide to play a game.

B The birds make wings for the bat.

C The mammals cannot catch the bat.

D The bat scores the winning points.

How does the way the bat flies help the birds?

2 Why do the birds win the game?

A The mammals cannot catch the bat.

B The bat flies in a straight line like the birds.

C The mammals refuse to play against a bat.

D The birds fly in a crazy, zigzag pattern.

What happens at the beginning of the story? How does each event lead to another event? How does the story end?

3 In your own words, recount the story "How the Bat Got Wings." Be sure to tell only the most important details of the story.

_____

_____

_____

_____

_____

_____

_____

_____

Read the folktale. Then answer the questions that follow.

True or False

a folktale from Myanmar (Burma)

1   There once were three poor brothers who loved to tell tall tales. They traveled throughout the countryside telling wild stories. They always claimed that their tales were true, but no one ever believed them.

2   One day, the three brothers met a rich traveler. The man was dressed in fine clothes and wore shining jewels. The brothers wanted his things. "Let's ask him to play a game. Each of the four of us will tell a tale of a past adventure. The rule is that if anyone doubts the truth of another's story, he must become that person's servant. The man will never believe our stories. Getting him to doubt our stories will be like rolling off a log. He will have to become our servant."

3   The others liked this plan. They did not want a servant. But they wanted the man's fine things. The man agreed to the game.

4   The first brother told a story of how he had climbed a tree and could not get down. So he ran to a nearby cottage and borrowed a rope.

5   The second brother told of jumping into the stomach of a tiger who wanted to eat him. "I made such a fuss that the tiger spit me out," he said.

6   The third told of helping the village fishermen. He said he turned into a fish and jumped into the river. There, he turned back into a man and killed the big fish that were eating all the little fish.

7   The rich man listened to the three tales without saying one word of disbelief. Then he told his story. He said he was searching for three servants who had run away from him.

8   "You three must be the ones I am looking for," he said.

9   The brothers looked at him with alarm. If they doubted him, they must become his servants. That was their rule. But if they said his story was true, they would have to become his servants too!

10   They said nothing.

11   Finally, the man said he would let them go if they promised never to tell tall tales again.

12   The brothers agreed, and they kept their promise.

Answer the questions. Mark your answers to questions 1–3 on the Answer Form to the right.

Answer Form

1 Ⓐ Ⓑ Ⓒ Ⓓ

2 Ⓐ Ⓑ Ⓒ Ⓓ   **Number**   /3

3 Ⓐ Ⓑ Ⓒ Ⓓ   **Correct**

1   Which is the **best** recounting of the game the brothers ask the rich man to play?

   A   Anybody who doubts a person's story must become that person's servant.

   B   Anybody who doubts a person's story must roll off of a log and into the water.

   C   Anybody who wants to play the game must be ready to give up their jewels if they lose.

   D   Anybody telling a tale does not have to become a servant.

2   Which is the **best** recounting of the third brother's story?

   A   He plays a trick on the fishermen by pretending to be a big fish catching small ones.

   B   He gets away from the fishermen by swimming in the river like a fish.

   C   He helps the fishermen by turning into a fish and then back into a person to kill a big fish.

   D   He becomes a fish so that he can help the fishermen chase fish into their nets.

3 Which is the **best** recounting of the brothers' problem at the end of the folktale?

   A The brothers are upset by the rich man's story.

   B The rich man believes that the brothers are the runaway servants he is looking for.

   C The brothers promise never to tell tall tales again.

   D No matter how the brothers answer the rich man, they will have to become his servants.

4 Recount the most important events in the folktale using your own words. Be sure to tell about the events in the order that they happen in the story.

_____

_____

_____

_____

_____

_____

_____

_____

_____

_____

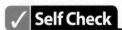 **Self Check** *Go back and see what you can check off on the Self Check on page 43.*

Lesson 8   Part 1: Introduction 👥
Determining the Central Message

CCSS
RL.3.2:...determine the central message, lesson, or moral and explain how it is conveyed through key details in the text.

Theme: *Tales of Wisdom*

Most stories have a **central message** the writer wants to share with readers. This "big idea" is often a **lesson** about life that the story teaches through the characters and the things that happen to them. Look for the **key details**, or the most important events, in a story to find the central message.

Look at the cartoon below. Think about the lesson the boy learns by the end.

Now look at the chart below. It shows how you can put together key details from the cartoon to find the central message or lesson. Complete the chart by finishing the sentence in the third column.

Key Detail in First Panel	Key Detail in Second Panel	Key Detail in Third Panel
The boy is worried about riding a bike by himself.	The girl lifts her hands off the bike while the boy is riding it.	The boy realizes he can _____ _____ _____.

Even though the boy is afraid at first, he learns that he can ride a bike by himself. Based on the key details in the cartoon, the central message is "Don't be afraid to try new things."

Good readers use the key details of a story to figure out the central message. The central message is often a lesson about life the author wants to share with readers.

Read the first part of a fable about a girl picking apples.

Genre: **Fable**

The Girl and the Apples   *by Tala Rutchel*

One fall afternoon, a girl went to a farm to pick apples. She was in a hurry so she picked carelessly, both ripe apples and unripe ones. When she finished, her wagon was filled with a small mountain of apples.

The girl asked the farmer, "Quick, tell me how long you think it will take me to get back home."

The farmer thought carefully. Then he said, "Be patient. If you go slow, you will be back soon. If you go fast, you will not get back until night. It's your choice."

The girl thought, "How can that be? How can it take so long if I go fast?"

(continued)

Explore how to answer this question: *"Based on the story so far, how do the key details hint at a lesson the girl might learn?"*

To answer this question, first look for key details about what the girl and the farmer say and do.

Write in the chart below some key details about what the characters say and do.

What the Girl Says and Does	What the Farmer Says and Does
• picks apples carelessly because she is in a _____ • wonders how it can take so long if she _____	• tells the girl to be patient • tells the girl that if she goes _____ , she will be home soon, but if she _____ , it will take longer • tells the girl "It's your choice."

Fill in the blanks to write how the key details suggest a lesson the girl might learn.

The farmer tells the girl that going _____ will get her home sooner

than going quickly, but that it is her _____ . The key details suggest the girl will learn

a lesson about making wise _____ .

Continue reading the fable about the girl and the apples. Use the Close Reading and the Hint to help you answer the question.

Close Reading

Does the girl follow the farmer's advice? **Underline** details that explain why hurrying home makes the girl's trip take longer.

(continued from page 70)

The girl wanted to get back home as soon as possible, so she rushed her horse and wagon onto the road. She made her horse walk very fast.

And suddenly . . . bump! Off fell some apples.

Every time she hit a bump, more apples rolled off her wagon. Then she had to stop and put them back on the wagon. Because of all the delays, it was night before she got home.

Hint

Why doesn't the girl arrive home until night?

Circle the correct answer.

What is the central message of "The Girl and the Apples"?

A Don't cry over spilled apples.

B Hurrying too much can actually waste time.

C Never give up in times of trouble.

D Listen to others but do what you think is best.

✎ **Show Your Thinking**

Look at the answer you chose. Write two details from the story that helped you choose that answer.

_____

_____

_____

_____

_____

 Imagine the girl had followed the farmer's advice. Talk with your partner about how this would change the central message of the story. What would that message be?

Read the folktale. Use the Study Buddy and the Close Reading to guide your reading.

I have to put together the most important details in order to find the central message. I'll start by rereading the story and thinking about which character learns a lesson.

Close Reading

What kind of deal does the land owner try to make with the farmer? **Draw a box** around the paragraph that explains this deal.

The land owner keeps changing his deal with the farmer. **Underline** a sentence that shows why he changes it.

Genre: **Folktale**

Sharing the Crops   *a folktale from England*

1   Once a farmer rented some land. "How much does it cost to use this land?" the farmer asked the land owner.

2   The owner, trying to get the better deal, said, "I'll take the top half of the crop, and you can take the bottom half."

3   So the clever farmer planted potatoes because they grow in the ground. At harvest time, he gave the owner the potato tops, which are not good for anything.

4   The owner knew he had been outsmarted. He said, "Next year, I want the bottom half of your crops."

5   So the next year the farmer planted oats, which grow at the top of long grasses. The farmer gave the bottom half— useless grassy straw—to the owner.

6   This time the owner said, "Next year, I'll take the top and the bottom. You can have the middle."

7   So this time, the farmer planted corn. At the top of each corn stalk are tassels. At the bottom are woody stalks. In the middle is where the tasty sweet corn grows.

8   For a third time, the owner had been outsmarted. Now it was the farmer's turn to suggest a deal. "From now on," he said, "why don't you take half of whatever I grow? Whatever I get, you will get the same."

9   This was a fair deal at last. From that day on, the owner and the farmer shared the crops equally.

Hints

Think about which character changes his ways at the end of the story.

Use the Hints to help you answer the questions.

1 Explain which character in "Sharing the Crops" learns a lesson. Use one detail from the folktale to support your response.

_____

_____

_____

_____

_____

_____

What does the land owner try to do in his deals with the farmer? Does it work?

2 What is the central message of "Sharing the Crops"?

A If you cheat others, they will cheat you.

B Never make a deal with a clever farmer.

C The best part of a crop is usually at the top.

D Farmers should plant different crops every year.

Look for a sentence that is directly related to the lesson the land owner learns.

3 Which sentence from the story best supports the answer you chose for question 2 above?

A "Once a farmer rented some land."

B "Now it was the farmer's turn to suggest a deal."

C "This was a fair deal at last."

D "So this time, the farmer planted corn."

Read the story. Then answer the questions that follow.

Zel, the Gentle Donkey

a folktale from Haiti

1   Long ago, there was a gentle donkey named Zel. Everyone in town loved Zel because she was so pleasant and kind. But Zel's owner, Madame Charity, was angry and mean. She was so mean that she threw rocks at birds for singing too loud. She yelled at little boys when they laughed. But she was the meanest of all to poor Zel.

2   Every Saturday, Madame Charity sold sugar and rice at a market. Whoever arrived earliest sold the most. But Madame Charity always woke up late. Then she got angry and yelled at Zel, who had done nothing wrong.

3   In a huff, Madame Charity would then load heavy bags of rice and sugar onto Zel's back. Last, she climbed on top of it. "Hurry, Zel!" she yelled. "Get me to market as fast as you can!" Although Zel always trotted as fast as she could, it was never fast enough for Madame Charity.

4   One day, Zel's friend Touloulou the crab visited. "Did you have a good day at the market?" asked Touloulou.

5   "Madame Charity was mad at me all day. I work as hard as I can, but she is always mean to me."

6   "Madame Charity is always late. She won't blame herself, so she blames you," said Touloulou.

7   "Yes," said Zel. "And because everyone is afraid of her angry tongue, she never sells much at the market."

8   "I will help you," said Touloulou.

9   The next Saturday, Madame Charity woke up at 9 A.M. "Oh, no! I'm late again!" she yelled. As she tossed her heavy bags onto Zel's back, Touloulou the crab grabbed onto the hem of her long skirt. Madame Charity climbed on Zel's back. Touloulou held tightly to her skirt.

10   Zel started trotting. Madame Charity remembered how late she was. She opened her mouth to speak angrily, but Touloulou pinched her ankle.

11   "Ouch!" Madame Charity rubbed her ankle. She forgot how late she was. But soon she remembered. "Faster, Zel! Faster!" she yelled.

12   Again Touloulou pinched Madame Charity's ankle.

13   "Ouch!" shouted Madame Charity.

14   When they got to the market, Madame Charity saw that someone had taken the stall she liked to use. In a fit of rage, Madame Charity opened her mouth to yell. For the third time, Touloulou pinched her ankle. Madame Charity screamed.

15   "What's wrong?" people asked.

16   "Hurrying to get to market, I must have hurt my ankle. It's very painful. Ouch! Ouch! Ouch!"

17   The fish seller said, "Madame Charity, you should get up earlier. Then you will not have to rush. Next week, I will wake you at 6 A.M."

18   "Thank you," said Madame Charity. She was surprised at the man's kindness.

19   "Let me fix your ankle," said the fruit seller. In the past, the fruit seller had not talked to Madame Charity. Today he felt sorry for her.

20   When Madame Charity saw how kind everyone was, she smiled. For the first time, she sold all of her rice and sugar. At the end of the day, she saddled Zel gently and rode quietly home.

21   From that day on, Madame Charity tried not to raise her voice in anger. Sometimes she got angry, but she kept it to herself. And Zel the gentle donkey was happy at last.

Part 5:

detail in the first part of the story explains
Madame Charity is mean to Zel?

1

A Zel does not walk to the market as fast as she is able to.

B Madame Charity is always angry about something.

C Madame Charity does not have enough sugar and rice to sell.

D Everyone in town loves Zel because she is pleasant and kind.

2 Describe how Touloulou helps Zel on the way to the market.

_____

_____

3 Which detail about Madame Charity is **most** important to the central message of the story?

A The fruit seller offers to wake her up at 6 A.M. the next week.

B She gets angry but only yells a little.

C She tries not to raise her voice in anger anymore.

D She feels sorry for Zel.

4 What is the central message of this story?

A Honesty is the best policy.

B Treat others as you want to be treated.

C Things are not always as they appear.

D Beware of strangers.

 **Self Check** *Go back and see what you can check off on the Self Check on page 43.*

Read the story. Then answer the questions that follow.

The Lost Camel

a folktale from India

1   There were once some merchants from across the ocean who traveled from place to place selling their wares. Late one evening as they made their way up the river, they lost one of their camels. They discovered he was missing when they stopped to make camp that night.

2   Early the next morning when they set out to look for him, they met a man coming along the road. They stopped and asked him if he had seen a camel. The man told them he had not seen the camel, but he was sure he could tell them where the camel was to be found. The merchants were puzzled by this, and they began to question the man. Was the camel carrying a load? they asked.

3   "Yes," the man answered. He was carrying bags of wheat on his left side and a large jar of honey on his right side. "Furthermore, the camel is blind in one eye and he has a missing tooth. But like I said, I haven't seen him. I can only tell you where you can find him."

4   "But you have given a perfect description of our lost camel!" the surprised merchants exclaimed.

5   "You probably have hidden our camel and intend to steal him!"

6   "I haven't seen him and I'm not a thief!" the man retorted. "But I have lived in this land a long time and there are some things I know!"

7   "Then tell us, how do you know he was carrying wheat and honey?" the merchants asked suspiciously.

8   "I know he was carrying wheat on his left side because grains had fallen along the left side of the path. The bag was probably cut by some branches. Ants were gathering the grains on the left side of the trail. I know he was carrying jars of honey because, on the right side of the path, flies were swarming where the honey had dripped."

9   "Fine, but how do you know he is blind in one eye?" the merchants asked.

10   "Because I noticed he had been grazing only on the right side of the path," the man answered.

11   "And how do you know he has a tooth missing?"

12   "Because where he had chewed the grass he left a clump in the middle of the bite. That told me he had a tooth missing."

13   "If the directions you give us are correct," the merchants said, "then we will reward you for the good news you have given us."

14   And so they went off to look for the camel, and they found him near the place where the man said he had seen the signs. They were very pleased to find their lost camel, and they rewarded the man who had been so clever.

Answer the questions. Mark your answers to questions 1–3 on the Answer Form to the right.

Answer Form

1 Ⓐ Ⓑ Ⓒ Ⓓ
2 Ⓐ Ⓑ Ⓒ Ⓓ   **Number**
3 Ⓐ Ⓑ Ⓒ Ⓓ   **Correct**   / 3

---

1   Why do the merchants think that the man they meet on the road is a thief?

   A   The man knows that a camel is missing from their camp.

   B   The man is carrying a bag of wheat and a jar of honey.

   C   The man tells them where to find the camel.

   D   The man gives them a perfect description of the camel.

2   How does the man know the camel is blind in one eye?

   A   The camel becomes lost in the dark night.

   B   The camel grazes on only one side of the path.

   C   The camel follows a path of ants back to camp.

   D   The camel is found not too far from the camp.

3 Which sentence from the story shows when the merchants learn the man is not a thief?

A "'I haven't seen him and I'm not a thief!' the man retorted."

B "And so they went off to look for the camel, and they found him near the place where the man said he had seen the signs."

C "The man told them he had not seen the camel, but he was sure he could tell them where the camel was to be found."

D "I know he was carrying wheat on his left side because grains had fallen along the left side of the path."

4 In a paragraph, tell the **most** important events in the story using your own words. Be sure to tell about the events in the order they happen.

_____

_____

_____

_____

5 In a paragraph, tell the central message of this story. Use **two** details from the story to support your answer.

_____

_____

_____

_____

Read the story. Then answer the questions that follow.

Real Treasure

by Pamela Walker, Highlights

1   When Grandma moved in with us, she brought a big trunk. I helped Dad put it at the end of Grandma's bed. It was heavy and looked like a treasure chest.

2   That first day, Grandma sat by the window and stared out. I don't know why. All she could see was the Johnsons' house next door.

3   The second day, I stood in her doorway until she looked at me. She asked me to come in.

4   "Are you sure?" I asked. "Mom said not to bother you."

5   "Oh, Aaron, that's silly. Come in here."

6   So I went in and straddled the trunk like I was riding a horse. "That's what I used to do when I was little!" She laughed and shook her head. "It's the funniest thing to see you sitting on it that way."

7   I was glad Grandma was laughing. "I thought this trunk might be a treasure chest," I told her.

8   "Full of rubies and gold!"

9   "Yeah, real treasure."

10   "You want to see what's inside?" she asked.

11   I hopped off, and she pulled her chair over to open the trunk. The oldest smells in the world floated out. Not bad, but not like everyday smells.

12   "See this letter? Your grandfather wrote this to me."

13   The paper was thin and kind of yellow. The writing was like the spidery veins on Grandma's hand.

14   "Is it a love letter?" I asked. It looked like it might be mushy.

15   "It sure is," she said.

16   Next, Grandma took out a little blue cup with a broken handle. "I once caught my brother using this teacup to dig fishing worms," she said, grinning. "I pounced on him like a wildcat!"

17   I tried to picture Grandma pouncing, but I couldn't see it.

18   Next, Grandma took out something wrapped in yellow cloth. It was a trophy of a girl riding a horse.

19   "You won that, Grandma?"

20   "Sure did. I won it riding Queen when I was 16 years old!"

21   Then she started putting things away. Her smile faded.

22   "You don't like it here, do you?" I blurted.

23   She rubbed her hands together and didn't say anything right away. "I don't dislike it," she said finally. "I guess I miss my window at home. I could picture every horse I'd ever owned—even Queen! I would see them out there running."

24   I looked out Grandma's window at the Johnsons' brick wall.

25   I went to my room and took out my art box. I used half a crayon to make the fields green. Then I drew horses.

26   While Grandma was in the kitchen the next morning, I taped the picture to her window. Some of the horses were eating grass. And some were running with their tails flying out behind them. Running fast, just like Queen.

Answer the questions. Mark your answers to questions 6–7B on the Answer Form to the right.

Answer Form

6 Ⓐ Ⓑ Ⓒ Ⓓ
7A Ⓐ Ⓑ Ⓒ Ⓓ   **Number** /3
7B Ⓐ Ⓑ Ⓒ Ⓓ   **Correct**

6   What does Grandma do on the first day she moves in with Aaron's family?

   A   She unpacks her big trunk.

   B   She draws pictures with Aaron.

   C   She sits by the window and looks out.

   D   She tells Aaron stories about Queen.

7 Answer Parts A and B below.

Part A

Based on "Real Treasure," how does Grandma feel about leaving her home?

A She wishes she had left her trophy behind.

B She misses looking out of her own window.

C She is glad to leave her old, lonely house.

D She is sad to be far away from her friends.

Part B

Which sentence from the story **best** shows Grandma's feelings about leaving home?

A "That first day, Grandma sat by the window and stared out."

B "She rubbed her hands together and didn't say anything right away."

C "I won it riding Queen when I was 16 years old!"

D "I guess I miss my window at home."

8 Explain why the things in the big trunk are important to Grandma. Use **two** details from the story to support your answer.

_____

_____

_____

_____

_____

Performance Task—Extended Response

9 At the end of the story, Aaron draws a picture and tapes it to his grandma's window. What makes Aaron want to do this for his grandma? Be sure to include details from the passage in your answer.

In your answer, be sure to
- tell why Aaron wants to draw a picture for his grandma
- describe the picture Aaron draws for his grandma
- use details from the passage in your answer

Check your writing for correct spelling, grammar, capitalization, and punctuation.

Use the space below to plan your essay.

Write your essay on the lines below.

_____

_____

_____

_____

_____

_____

_____

_____

_____

_____

_____

_____

_____

_____

_____

_____

How is a writer like a carpenter and an artist? Well, just like carpenters and artists, writers have special tools. They use these tools to help them do their jobs. Carpenters use hammers and nails to build things. Artists use paints and brushes to make paintings. And writers use words in special ways. For example, words in **bold print** or in a box in a passage stand out to help readers find information. Writers can also provide word clues to help readers figure out difficult words. And some words tell opinions to help readers know how the writer feels about a topic. All of these word tools help readers search for and use information in a passage.

In this unit, you'll practice using word clues to figure out new words. You'll learn to use special parts of the text to look for information. And you'll see that understanding how writers view their topics can help you build your own views about what you read. So, be on the lookout for word tools!

✓ Self Check

Before starting this unit, check off the skills you know below. As you complete each lesson, see how many more you can check off!

I know how to:	Before this unit	After this unit
look for word clues to help me find the meanings of new words.	☐	☐
use special parts of a passage, such as titles and headings, to find information.	☐	☐
use special parts of a passage, such as sidebars, key words, and hyperlinks to find information.	☐	☐
discover how a writer thinks or feels about what they have written.	☐	☐
decide how I think or feel about what I read.	☐	☐

Lesson 9   Part 1: Introduction 👥
Unfamiliar Words

CCSS
RI.3.4: Determine the meaning of general academic and domain-specific words and phrases in a text relevant to a grade 3 topic or subject area.

Theme: *Animal Helpers*

You can often figure out the meaning of a word by seeing how it is used in a sentence or paragraph. Such **context clues**, along with what you already know about a topic, can help you figure out what a word means.

Some words have a special meaning when they are used in texts about certain subjects. For example, in a science passage about bears, you might read the word *hibernate*, which means "to spend the winter in a sleeping state."

Read the paragraph below about cats in ancient Egypt.

> Cats played an essential role in ancient Egypt. They were prized pets. But they were also useful. For example, cats killed dangerous snakes. They caught mice and rats to protect stores of grain. Some cats even helped gather food. Egyptian hunters trained them to bring back birds and fish from the marshes.

Now read the paragraph again. This time, circle any words you don't know.

Were there any words you didn't know? The word *essential* in the first sentence might have been one. Context clues can help you figure out the meaning of *essential*.

Read the chart below. It shows one way to figure out the meaning of *essential*.

Unknown Word: *Essential*		
Context Clues	**What I Already Know**	**What the Word Means**
• cats killed dangerous snakes • cats helped protect grain • cats helped gather food	• Some animals can be trained to help people. • It's very important to find and protect food and to keep people safe.	The word *essential* means "very important."

When you don't know the meaning of a word, look around in the text for context clues. They will help you figure out what the word means. The more words you know, the more you will enjoy and understand what you read.

Read the first part of a social studies passage about reading therapy dogs.

Genre: **Social Studies**

Woof! Woof! Read Me a Story   *by Kara Williams*

Dogs cannot read. But they can help children who may not like to read, or who find reading difficult. Reading therapy dogs and their owners visit schools and libraries. While sitting on the floor, a child reads aloud a story to the dog. The dog helps the child relax. It offers the child support and encouragement.

Only some dogs can be reading therapy dogs. First, dogs are tested to make sure they are calm and friendly. They have to be able to handle different situations. Then the dogs are trained to be patient listeners. Some even learn how to turn the pages of a book with their noses or paws.

(continued)

Explore how to answer this question: *"In this passage, what do the words* therapy dogs *mean?"*

Look for clues in the passage to understand what the words *therapy dogs* mean. In the table below, we've listed two clues for you.

Write a third clue in the "Clues" column. Then fill in the blank in the "What the Words Mean" column.

Clues from the Passage	What I Already Know	What the Words Mean
• Reading therapy dogs "help children who may not like to read, or who find reading difficult." • Therapy dogs help a child relax. • _____ _____ _____ _____	• Dogs help people in many different ways. • Dogs can be trained to do different things.	*Therapy dogs* are dogs that have special training to help others. This passage tells about therapy dogs that are trained to help children _____ .

Continue reading the passage about reading therapy dogs. Use the Close Reading and the Hint to help you answer the question below.

Close Reading

Look carefully at the first and last sentences of this paragraph. **Circle** two words that tell how therapy dogs help children.

(continued from page 88)

Studies show that reading therapy dogs can enhance reading skills. The dogs encourage children to practice reading without being afraid of making mistakes. Shy readers gain confidence. As children begin to feel better about their reading, they enjoy reading more. The more that children read, the more their reading ability improves.

Hint

What do you already know about reading therapy dogs? How do they help people?

Circle the correct answer.

Which word from the passage best helps the reader understand what the word *enhance* means?

A "afraid"

B "mistakes"

C "practice"

D "improves"

 Show Your Thinking

Look at the answer that you chose above. Explain how the context clues in the passage help the reader figure out the meaning of *enhance*.

_____

_____

_____

_____

Choose another word or a group of words in the passage that helps you figure out the meaning of *enhance*. Discuss this word with your partner.

Read the science passage. Use the Study Buddy and Close Reading to guide your reading.

Genre: **Science**

Because this is a science passage, there might be some science words I don't know. I'm going to circle any words that are new to me.

Close Reading

How do scientists train bees and wasps to smell certain things? **Underline** sentences that explain what scientists do to train bees and wasps.

Which words in paragraph 4 give you clues about the meaning of *detect*? **Circle** these words.

The Buzz on Sniffer Bees and Wasps
by Heather Robertson

1   Did you know that bees and wasps have a great sense of smell? The antennae, or feelers, on their heads have more than three thousand tiny smell organs. With their antennae, bees and wasps can identify more than 170 different odors. This is how they locate food, water, and pollen.

2   These insects have a much better sense of smell than people do. They can sniff out scents that humans cannot. For this reason, scientists are researching some practical ways that trained bees and wasps can assist humans.

3   Scientists can teach bees and wasps to recognize specific smells. First, the bees or wasps are given a target smell. When they move toward the same smell in another area, they are rewarded with sugar water. Scientists repeat this process until the insects connect that smell with a treat.

4   Sniffer bees and wasps have been trained to detect harmful materials. For example, they can sniff out certain health problems. They can uncover some kinds of cancer. They can recognize a lung disease called tuberculosis (too ber kyoo LOW sis). They can also smell dangerous chemicals. In addition, they can find out plant diseases or pests like bedbugs.

5   One day, these tiny helpers may work in airports, farms, hospitals, and war zones. They will alert humans to possible danger in these places.

Hints

Use the Hints on this page to help you answer the questions.

1 Explain the meaning of *antennae* as it is used in this passage. Use clues in the first paragraph to find the meaning of this word. Include two details from the passage to support your response.

_____

_____

_____

_____

2 Read this sentence from the passage.

> Scientists repeat this process until the insects connect that smell with a treat.

What is the meaning of *process* as it is used in this sentence?

A a series of actions taken for a certain purpose

B a reward for having done something correctly

C something that can happen only once

D a secret way of training something to like chemicals

3 Read this sentence from the passage.

> Sniffer bees and wasps have been trained to detect harmful materials.

What is the meaning of *detect*?

A change

B help

C discover

D frighten

Read the social studies article. Then answer the questions that follow.

from "Horses Helping Others"

by Natasha Yim, Appleseeds

1   In 1993, when Erin Livingston was just 11, she had an idea. She wanted to use horses to help kids with special needs. Along with two friends, she researched different programs. With the support of the Mendocino County 4-H, Ridgewood T.R.A.I.L.[1] was born.

2   Freya, Kiss, Easy, Ginger, and Robin are horses with a very important job. They help kids with special needs. Some of these kids are in wheelchairs and walkers. Some can't talk. Some are very high energy and need to learn how to focus.

3   Erin uses games to help kids learn to communicate with horses. For example, a rope is attached to the halter of a horse. The student holds the other end and wiggles it to make the horse back up. Then the student wiggles it again to invite the horse back into his or her space.

4   Through interactive games, the horses help the kids learn about trust, keeping themselves safe, and being sensitive to a horse's feelings and body language. If kids are loud and too full of energy, the horse may not want to come over to them.

5   "The kids learn to protect their space, and also to invite the horse into their space," says Erin Livingston, the founder of Ridgewood T.R.A.I.L.

6   For a child who can't walk, riding works her leg muscles. A horse's walking motion is very similar to our own hip movements. Children who have a hard time staying on task learn to pay attention. If they turn to the left when they want to go right, the horse may not do what they want it to do. For a kid who has a hard time talking, Erin has her use words to command the horse. One boy uttered his first sentence, "Walk on, Woody" while riding a horse! Another student is now a helper in the program. "She has so much confidence and pride in what she does," says her mother.

[1] **T.R.A.I.L.:** Teaching Riding as an Access to Independence and Learning

7   "We focus on the kids' abilities, not their disabilities," Erin says.

8   Good program horses are calm, patient, and understanding. They have to be used to people (there could be up to two or three helpers walking alongside a rider), loud noises, and sudden movements. It's exhausting work. But the next day, they're back at it, patient as ever—just another day at the office for these amazing horses!

Answer the questions. Mark your answers to questions 1–4 on the Answer Form to the right.

Answer Form

1 Ⓐ Ⓑ Ⓒ Ⓓ
2 Ⓐ Ⓑ Ⓒ Ⓓ
3 Ⓐ Ⓑ Ⓒ Ⓓ   **Number**
4 Ⓐ Ⓑ Ⓒ Ⓓ   **Correct** /4

1   What is the meaning of the word "interactive" in paragraph 4?

   A   acting apart from each other

   B   acting too closely together

   C   acting in response to each other

   D   acting politely together

2   Read this sentence from the article.

   Erin uses games to help kids learn to communicate with horses.

   Which word from the article has the same meaning as "communicate"?

   A   talk

   B   focus

   C   invite

   D   wiggle

3   What is the meaning of the word "sensitive" in paragraph 4?

    A   unfeeling

    B   understanding

    C   fearful

    D   amazed

4   Read these sentences from paragraph 6 of the passage.

> For a kid who has a hard time talking, Erin has her use words to command the horse. One boy uttered his first sentence, "Walk on, Woody" while riding a horse!

    What does the word "uttered" mean in paragraph 6?

    A   spoke

    B   wrote

    C   understood

    D   heard

5   In paragraph 7, Erin states, "We focus on the kids' abilities, not their disabilities." Explain what "disabilities" means. Support your response with **two** details from the passage.

    _____

    _____

    _____

    _____

    ✓ **Self Check**   *Go back and see what you can check off on the Self Check on page 85.*

Lesson 10 Part 1: Introduction 👥

Text Features

CCSS

RI.3.5: Use text features and search tools (e.g., key words, sidebars, hyperlinks) to locate information relevant to a given topic efficiently.

Theme: *How Nature Adapts*

Text features are special parts of a passage that organize information for readers. You can use text features to quickly locate facts and details in a passage.

Read the passage below. It has many text features that organize the information.

Long Live the Lungfish

If you had to be a fish, you might want to be a lungfish. Why? Because the lungfish can do some amazing things that most other fish cannot.

A Fish out of Water

The lungfish can breathe air. If its lake or river dries up, the lungfish drags itself over land until it finds water in which to live.

A Fish Under Ground

If the lungfish can't find water to live in, it digs a hole in the ground and sleeps there until the water returns. This type of sleep is called **estivation**.

Fun Facts

- Lungfish live in South America, Australia, and Africa.
- Lungfish can live for more than 80 years.
- Lungfish have been around since *before* the dinosaurs.

If you want to learn more about lungfish, visit our website: www.ilovelungfish.org.

Now read the chart. Use it to label one example of each text feature in the passage.

Text Feature	Purpose
Title	tells what the whole passage is about
Heading	tells what a specific part of a passage is about
Key word	calls attention to an important word using bold print
Sidebar	gives more details related to the main topic by boxing or highlighting information
Hyperlink	takes readers to information in another location, such as a website: http://www.pbskids.org

Learning how to use text features will help you find facts about a topic quickly. It is a skill that every good reader learns over time.

Read the first part of a science passage about polar bears.

Brrr . . . Polar Bears in the Arctic   by Devonte Thomas

Polar bears live in the Arctic. The Arctic is one of the coldest places on Earth. How do polar bears survive in the ice and snow?

Built for Living in the Arctic

Polar bears have thick, white fur. The outer layer of fur is made of oily, hollow **guard hairs**. These hairs keep the bears dry. The inner layer of fur next to their skin acts like a sweater. It traps in heat and keeps them warm. Under their fur, polar bears have a thick layer of fat. Also, polar bears have black skin and black noses. The color black **absorbs**, or takes in, more of the sun's heat.

(continued)

Explore how to answer this question: *"Which text features help you find details about how polar bears survive in the Arctic?"*

Look for text features that help you search for information about how polar bears survive.

One example is listed in the chart. Write two more examples on the lines.

Text Feature	Example from the Passage	Purpose in the Passage
Heading	_____ _____	tells what paragraph 2 of the passage is mostly about
Key words	guard hairs, _____	calls attention to words that are important to the topic

How do these text features help you find details about how polar bears survive in the Arctic?

Fill in the blanks below to write about text features in this passage.

The heading _____ tells me that this part is about

how polar bears have special bodies for living in the Arctic. The key words _____

and _____ help me locate details about how polar bears survive in the Arctic.

Continue reading about polar bears. Use the Close Reading and the Hint to help you answer the question below.

Close Reading

Which text features do you see in this part of the passage? Find and **circle** the text features.

(continued from page 96)

Behavior

Polar bears have other ways to cope with the cold. They stay in a **den** all winter. Their body functions slow down. They do not eat or drink. For more polar bear facts, go to this website: http://www. polarbearsinternational.org.

Fast Facts Sidebar
Baby, It's Cold Outside! The Arctic is a cold, snowy region around the North Pole. In winter, the temperature can drop as low as −40°F.

Hint

What do you learn from each text feature in this passage?

Circle the correct answer.

Where in this passage can you find information about Arctic weather?

A   the heading

B   the key words

C   the sidebar

D   the hyperlink

✎ Show Your Thinking

Look at the answer that you chose above. Describe the information in this text feature.

_____

_____

_____

_____

 Pick one answer you did not choose. Tell your partner why this answer is not a text feature that helps you learn about Arctic weather.

Read the science passage. Use the Study Buddy and Close Reading to guide your reading.

Genre: **Science**

How Plants Live in a Desert
by Rafael Sanchez

1   A desert gets less than 10 inches of rain per year. It can get as hot as 100 degrees in the summer. Yet at night, it can be quite cold. It's not easy to live in a desert, but some plants do.

Cactus Plants

2   Many cactuses have a waxy coating. The wax helps keep water in the cactus by preventing it from **evaporating**, or escaping through tiny holes in the plant. Cactuses are good at storing water. When it rains, a cactus stores water to live on during dry periods. For more information on cactus plants, go to http://www.desertmuseum.org/kids/oz/long-fact-sheets/.

Plants with Long Roots

3   A second type of desert plant, such as the **mesquite** (meh SKEET) tree, grows very long roots. These roots find water deep in the ground. Some mesquites have roots that are 80 feet long!

Plants with Hardy Seeds

4   A third type of plant grows only in the spring, following winter rains. It grows quickly. Soon it drops seeds. These seeds can live for a long time. If the following spring is wet, the seeds will grow. If not, the seeds may wait two or three springs to grow.

> **Deserts Around the Globe**
> There are many deserts around the world. The Sahara Desert is in Africa. The Gobi Desert is in Asia. The Great Basin and Mojave (moh HAHV ee) deserts stretch across the American Southwest.

I'm going to look at the headings and key words to quickly find out if this passage has information about desert plants with seeds that live a long time.

Close Reading

Which text features point you to information about plants that have long roots? **Underline** each of these text features.

What information do you learn from reading the sidebar? **Draw a box** around this text feature.

Hints

What type of text feature directs you to information found in another location?

Review the chart of text features and their purposes on page 95. Then look back at the text features you underlined in "How Plants Live in a Desert."

What facts and details do you learn from reading the sidebar?

Use the Hints on this page to help you answer the questions.

1 Which text feature would be most useful for finding out more about cactus plants?

   A the hyperlink at the end of paragraph 2

   B the sidebar "Deserts Around the Globe"

   C the key word *mesquite* in paragraph 3

   D the heading "Plants with Hardy Seeds"

2 Name a desert plant that has very long roots. Then tell which two text features in the passage helped you locate this information.

Type of desert plant that has very long roots:

_____

_____

First text feature that helped me find this information:

_____

_____

_____

Second text feature that helped me find this information:

_____

_____

_____

3 By reading the sidebar in this passage, you can find out about

   A plants in the Sahara Desert.

   B plants in cool, wet climates.

   C deserts around the world.

   D different kinds of cactus.

Read the science article. Then answer the questions that follow.

from "Crazy Critters"

by Fran Downy and Peter Winkler, National Geographic Explorer

1   Some animals look really crazy! Their odd looks fit their wild lives perfectly.

2   How do creatures last in the wild? They have **adaptations**. These are things that allow an animal to live. Sometimes, adaptations are body parts. Other times, they can be ways of acting.

3   Long ears are adaptations. Big bills and blue feet are too. So are running, jumping, and flying. Most adaptations seem normal. Others look odd. They all allow creatures to live.

4   Now let's meet some animals that look crazy. We will see how their strange looks help them live in the wild.

Extra Eye

5   We will start with the very rare tuatara (too ah TAH rah). It lives on small islands in New Zealand. That is a country in the Pacific Ocean.

6   The tuatara looks like a lizard. Yet it is not. Lizards have ears. It does not. Lizards like warmth. It does not. Lizards come out during the day. It does not.

7   This animal is a bit odd. You see, it has a **third eye**. The eye sits on the top of the animal's head.

Two Tuataras

8   What does this adaptation do? We do not really know. It may help with seeing in the dark. Or it may help the animal tell time or the season.

Using Their Heads

9   The hornbill also has an odd head. The bird looks like it is wearing a hat! It is made of the same stuff as the nails on your fingers and toes.

10   The hat might help the bird make noise. It may also help support the bird's long **bill**. The bird uses its big mouth to eat fruit.

11   The chameleon has an odd head too. It holds a tongue that stretches longer than the animal's body!

12   A chameleon uses its tongue to catch dinner. The animal likes to eat bugs, birds, and other lizards. It flicks its tongue at prey. It then pulls the prey into its mouth.

Crazy Colors

13   Color helps animals in many ways. Mandrills are monkeys in western Africa. The males have bright red noses. They have blue cheeks. The females like those colors. They pick males with the most colorful faces.

14   The mandarin (man duh rihn) fish lives in the Pacific Ocean. It is blue, green, orange, and yellow. The males show off their colors. The colors make a big splash with the females.

15   The zorilla of Africa is mostly black. It has white **stripes** on its back. Other animals know this animal by color. They see the zorilla's stripes as a warning. Zorillas make an awful smell when they are in trouble. The smell keeps this animal safe.

Forever Young

16   Now it's time to meet one of the oddest animals. It's a salamander. Most salamanders are born in water. They grow up and move onto land. Not the axolotl (ax oh lot ul).

17   It never grows up. It spends its whole life in Mexican lakes. Pink **gills** help it breathe.

18   What caused this adaptation? No one knows for sure. Yet this strange animal does well in the wild. How? Adaptations, of course!

> **Cool Chameleon Facts**
> - A chameleon's tongue can hit a bug in just one-sixteenth of a second.
> - A chameleon can move each eye separately. It can look backward and forward at the same time!

1 Which heading would be **most** helpful for finding facts about animals with oddly shaped heads?

A Extra Eye

B Using Their Heads

C Crazy Colors

D Forever Young

Answer Form

1 Ⓐ Ⓑ Ⓒ Ⓓ
2 Ⓐ Ⓑ Ⓒ Ⓓ   **Number**
3 Ⓐ Ⓑ Ⓒ Ⓓ   **Correct** /3

2 What can you learn more about by reading the sidebar in this article?

   A salamanders

   B tuataras

   C chameleons

   D mandarin fish

3 Which text feature helps you understand why the axolotl is odd?

   A the key word "**stripes**"

   B the heading "Extra Eye"

   C the key word "**gills**"

   D the title "Crazy Critters"

4 Name one animal in the article that uses color to help it survive in the wild. Then tell what text feature in this article helped you find this information.

Name one animal that uses color to help it survive in the wild.

_____

Tell what text feature in the passage helped you find this information.

_____

_____

_____

 **✓ Self Check** *Go back and see what you can check off on the Self Check on page 85.*

Lesson 11 Part 1: Introduction

Author's Point of View

CCSS

RI.3.6: Distinguish their own point of view from that of the author of a text.

Theme: *Works of Art*

What is your point of view about hip-hop music? Do your friends agree with you? Your **point of view** is the way you think or feel about something. Your friends may feel the same way or have different ideas. Not everyone will share your point of view about hip-hop music—or about other ideas, either. How boring would that be?

Look at the cartoon below. How does each person feel about the loud music?

Read through the chart below. Complete it by telling the father's point of view.

Person	Details	Point of View
Boy	• smiles • turns up sound	enjoys the loud music
Father	• covers his ears • calls the music noise	_____ _____

How do *you* feel about loud music? Which character most closely shares your point of view?

_____

Authors often give their points of view about topics they explain or describe. They do this by using opinion words such as *best, worst, beautiful, like, dislike, feel,* and *believe.* As you read, try to figure out the author's feelings by noticing these types of word clues. Then form your own point of view about the topic.

Read the start of a review to learn about the author's point of view on a sculpture.

Genre: **Review**

Make Way for the Mallard Family   *by Jessie Green*

Make Way for Ducklings is a children's book by Robert McCloskey. In it, a mother and her eight ducklings walk to a park in Boston, Massachusetts. Today, a delightful bronze sculpture of Mrs. Mallard and her ducklings stands in Boston's Public Garden. Almost as popular as the book, this treasured landmark seems to bring the duck family to life!

Nancy Schön made this charming creation in 1987. It is a series of nine adorable statues. Mrs. Mallard, Jack, Quack, and the other ducklings proudly parade in a row. Children touch, pet, and cuddle these life-like statues so often that they never need to be polished.

(continued)

Explore how to answer this question: *"What is the author's point of view about the sculpture of Mrs. Mallard and her ducklings?"*

The author does not directly tell you how she feels about the sculpture. But you can look for word clues in the review to figure out her point of view about her topic.

Complete the chart. Add opinion words that the author uses to describe the sculpture. Two word clues are provided for you. Write two more clues in the left column.

Words Describing the Sculpture	Author's Point of View on the Sculpture
• "delightful bronze sculpture" • "treasured landmark" • _____ • _____	She admires, or truly likes, the sculpture.

In your own words, write about the author's point of view on the sculpture. Explain how words such as "treasured landmark" help you figure out her feelings. Use the chart for help.

_____

_____

_____

Continue reading the review. Use the Close Reading and the Hint to help you answer the question.

Close Reading

Circle opinion words and phrases that help you understand the author's point of view about the person who took Pack.

(continued from page 104)

A greedy thief stole Pack, one of the ducklings, in 2009. The cowardly criminal snapped the bird off at its webbed feet. This senseless attack angered many people. Boston's Mayor Menino said, "This act is not a prank, it is a crime."

Fortunately, the missing statue was found four blocks away. It was leaning against a tree. The surprised residents who found the stolen duckling returned it immediately. Soon, Pack was back where he belonged, waddling in the parade.

Hint

What do the words you circled in the passage tell about the author's feelings?

Circle the correct answer.

What is the author's point of view on the person who took Pack?

A She thinks this person is worried.

B She thinks this person is thoughtful.

C She thinks this person is mean.

D She thinks this person is clever.

✎ Show Your Thinking

What is your point of view about the sculpture of Mrs. Mallard and the ducklings? Is it similar to or different from the author's point of view? Use details from the passage to tell why.

_____

_____

_____

_____

 With a partner, share your point of view about the person who took Pack. Use details from the passage to tell how your feelings are similar to or different from the author's point of view.

105

Read the review. Use the Study Buddy and the Close Reading to guide your reading.

Since this passage is a review, it will give the author's point of view about the contest. As I read, I'll figure out his feelings, and I'll also form my own opinions.

Genre: **Review**

Snow Sculpture Contest   *by Kim Wu*

1   The town of Butler hosted its first Winter Fest this week. The highlight of the outdoor event was the snow sculpture contest. Teams of snow carvers worked tirelessly to create remarkable works of art that delighted the crowds.

2   Snow sculpture is a very difficult kind of sculpture to make. Teams of snow carvers made impressive sculptures from huge blocks of snow. Each team used only hand tools, such as shovels and cheese graters. For a whole day, they cut away packed snow from the heavy blocks. By late afternoon, these snow artists had created amazing sculptures. Some of the snow sculptures were nine feet tall!

3   My favorite snow sculpture won second prize. This sculpture of a giant dragon looked fierce. It had detailed scales, a pair of giant wings, and a long tail. How funny that the dragon breathed fire made of snow!

4   The snow sculpture that won third prize was a good choice by the judges. It was a copy of the White House in Washington, D.C.

5   I didn't like the snow sculpture that captured first prize. It was a covered wagon. The team of carvers made the wagon wheels too small! They made other mistakes, too.

6   I was disappointed that my favorite sculpture did not win the grand prize. But Butler's first Winter Fest was still a great success. The weather was perfect. I can't wait to see more amazing snow sculptures at Winter Fest next year!

Close Reading

Why doesn't Kim Wu like the sculpture that won first prize? **Circle** sentences that explain why he didn't like this sculpture.

What is Kim Wu's opinion of Winter Fest? **Underline** sentences that give clues about his point of view.

Hints

Reread the paragraph to look for details about making snow sculptures. Also find word clues about the author's point of view.

Use the Hints on this page to help you answer the questions.

1 In the second paragraph, the author says, "Snow sculpture is a very difficult kind of sculpture to make." Explain whether or not you agree. Compare your opinion with Kim Wu's point of view.

_____

_____

_____

_____

_____

_____

_____

_____

Which statement best tells Kim Wu's feelings about a prize winner in the contest?

2 Which sentence from the review best describes the author's point of view on the results of the snow sculpture contest?

   A "The town of Butler hosted its first Winter Fest this week."

   B "Some of the snow sculptures were nine feet tall!"

   C "It was a copy of the White House in Washington, D.C."

   D "I didn't like the snow sculpture that captured first prize."

How does Kim Wu feel about Winter Fest?

3 With which statement would the author most likely agree?

   A Butler should hold another Winter Fest.

   B Butler should not hold another Winter Fest.

   C Winter Fest was crowded with tourists.

   D Winter Fest did not have enough activities.

Read the article about a symbol of freedom. Then answer the questions that follow.

from "Our Most Famous Immigrant"

by Nancy Whitelaw, Cobblestone

1   America's most famous immigrant arrived here in 1885. She was packed in 214 boxes. She was about 10 years old then. America had been waiting nine years for her. She was the Statue of Liberty. Her story begins long ago in France.

Statue of Liberty, Liberty Island, New York City

2   It is April 1876. Frederic Auguste Bartholdi, a French sculptor, has a problem. He has been commissioned to complete a statue as a gift from France to America for America's 100th birthday.

3   "July fourth, July fourth," he mutters over and over. "It can't be done."

4   Plaster dust swirls through the air around the partly finished statue. Gobs of wet plaster fall in heaps on the floor below it. Workmen climb up and down the scaffolds, hauling pails of materials and tools.

5   The noise is deafening. Men are shouting directions. Saws are rasping at ragged edges. Mallets are clanging copper sheets into molds. Hammers are nailing wood strips together.

6   An idea comes to Bartholdi. "I'll finish the arm and torch. I'll send them in time for the 4th of July so the Americans can at least imagine the whole statue." This is no small present. The hand alone is 16 feet high.

7   When the arm and torch finally are completed, Bartholdi has them shipped to the Philadelphia World's Fair. The Americans are amazed and delighted. The sculptor feels some relief that his art is appreciated. But he still has a great deal of work to do to finish building the world's largest statue.

8   Finally, in 1884, she stands tall and proud. She looks over the rooftops of Paris, France. She stays there until January 1885, while the Americans build a pedestal for her. Then, Bartholdi orders his crew to dismantle the statue and pack her into boxes.

9　　Two hundred fourteen boxes arrive at Bedloe's Island in New York Harbor on June 17, 1885. A reporter opens some of the boxes. "I found one case that had just the eyebrows and forehead," he writes. "Another contained the left ear and some pieces of hair. One box that was eight feet long held one of her curls." Workmen in America assemble the statue—all 216 feet of her—on an 89-foot-tall pedestal.

10　　On October 18, 1886, crowds of cheering spectators gather at the shore to watch the unveiling. The 300 boats in the harbor clear a path to the statue for President Grover Cleveland and his party. Bartholdi, positioned high in the torch of the statue, pulls the cord to unveil the face of the statue called *Liberty Enlightening the World*. Thousands cheer, wave banners, blow whistles, sound sirens, beat drums, and ring bells.

Answer the questions. Mark your answers to questions 1–3 on the Answer Form to the right.

Answer Form

1　Ⓐ　Ⓑ　Ⓒ　Ⓓ
2　Ⓐ　Ⓑ　Ⓒ　Ⓓ　　**Number**
3　Ⓐ　Ⓑ　Ⓒ　Ⓓ　　**Correct**　　╱3

1　Which sentence from the article **best** describes the author's point of view on the Statue of Liberty?

　　A　"Her story begins long ago in France."

　　B　"Saws are rasping at ragged edges."

　　C　"Finally, in 1884, she stands tall and proud."

　　D　"A reporter opens some of the boxes."

2　With which statement would the author of this article **most likely** agree?

　　A　The Statue of Liberty has a fun and interesting history.

　　B　The Statue of Liberty took 100 years to finish.

　　C　The Statue of Liberty should have been much taller.

　　D　The Statue of Liberty cost too much money to make.

3 Read these sentences from paragraph 10 of the article.

> Bartholdi, positioned high in the torch of the statue, pulls the cord to unveil the face of the statue called *Liberty Enlightening the World*. Thousands cheer, wave banners, blow whistles, sound sirens, beat drums, and ring bells.

Which word **best** describes the author's point of view on the 1886 unveiling of the Statue of Liberty?

A disappointed

B confused

C upset

D excited

4 An immigrant is a person who comes to a country to live there. In paragraph 1, the author calls the Statue of Liberty "America's most famous immigrant." Explain whether or not you agree. Compare your opinion with Nancy Whitelaw's point of view. Use **two** details from the article to support your response.

_____

_____

_____

_____

_____

_____

_____

 **Self Check** *Go back and see what you can check off on the Self Check on page 85.*

Read the article. Then answer the questions that follow.

Big Bugs

by Jennifer Martox, Highlights

1   Imagine walking through the park on a sunny day. You look up to see a spider twice the size of your head. It looks so real that it seems to be creeping down its web toward you.

2   Before you scream and run away, look closer. That 50-pound spider is a wood sculpture. It was made by artist David Rogers and is one of 14 bugs he has on display in parks and gardens around the United States.

Ants the Size of a Bus!

3   David's collection is called Big Bugs. It includes three monster ants. Each one stretches 25 feet long. That's almost as long as a school bus! The collection also includes a praying mantis that weighs 1,200 pounds. How heavy is that? It would be like picking up six grown men at once. Some of David's other bugs are a grasshopper, an assassin bug, and a ladybug— all big enough to sit on.

> It's hard to ignore an ant that's almost as long as a school bus.

4   Real bugs are tiny. So why did David build his so large?

5   David hopes his jumbo sculptures will help us to stop and notice bugs. We may not see them working. Sometimes we may not even want them around. But David points out that bugs are an important part of nature. They make the soil a better place for plants to grow, they pollinate flowers, they eat other insects, and they are food to many creatures.

Bugs Under Construction

6   Making such massive art is not easy. Some of the bugs took three months to construct.

7   David began by carving pieces of wood into just the right shape and size. He used a mix of black walnut, red cedar, and black locust woods to craft each bug. He also used young willow trees to show texture in his ladybug and ants.

8   He then connected the parts using metal rods. Finally, he gave them a coat of varnish for a smooth, shiny finish.

Sticks and Strings

9   As a child, David Rogers did not get the best grades. He was not even the best painter. But he loved to make things. Using only sticks and string, he would build tiny villages small enough for an insect.

10   One day when he was older, he saw a bent tree that reminded him of the backbone of an animal. He decided to form a giant beast by adding more branches. The result was a dinosaur named Goliath. Goliath was his first large sculpture.

11   David has also made sculptures by welding metal. By joining together old car parts, he made a housefly and a dragonfly. Does this sound like fun to you? Good news—David believes there's an artist in everyone.

12   Of course, you probably won't start out by making a 25-foot ant. It took David years to come up with his huge bugs. But as David says, "There's no right or wrong way to express yourself with art. Let your imagination run free."

Answer the questions. Mark your answers to questions 1–2B on the Answer Form to the right.

Answer Form

1   Ⓐ Ⓑ Ⓒ Ⓓ
2A Ⓐ Ⓑ Ⓒ Ⓓ **Number** **3**
2B Ⓐ Ⓑ Ⓒ Ⓓ **Correct**

1   Which is the **best** place to find information about how the artist built his bug art?

   A   under the heading "Ants the Size of a Bus!"

   B   under the heading "Bugs Under Construction"

   C   the sidebar

   D   the photographs

2 Answer Parts A and B below.

Part A

What does the word "monster" mean as it is used in the passage?

A huge

B silly

C unsafe

D strong

Part B

Which of the phrases from the passage **best** helps the reader understand the meaning of "monster"?

A "big enough to sit on"

B "weighs 1,200 pounds"

C "like picking up six grown men"

D "almost as long as a school bus"

3 Based on the passage, describe the author's point of view on Big Bug art. Use **two** details from the passage to support your answer.

_____

_____

_____

_____

_____

Read the science passage. Then answer the questions that follow.

The Praying Mantid

by Stephanie Petrie

1   This insect looks like a thin green or brown stick with two large eyes. The eyes are set on either side of its head. It has the amazing ability to turn its head almost a full 180 degrees. That's a full half circle. It gets its name from the way its two front legs are bent. It looks as if it were kneeling and praying. Most people call this insect a "praying mantis." But its real name is the "praying mantid."

What They Eat

2   Praying mantids are **carnviores**—they eat other small animals and insects. They like to eat moths, grasshoppers, and flies. Some even like to eat lizards, frogs, and spiders. Farmers like mantids because they help them by eating insects that could hurt their crops. Gardeners also like mantids. Mantids help them by eating pesky insects that eat their fruit and flowers. Mantids are very helpful to people. Every garden should have a few of their own! When a mantid grows to an adult, it has to watch out that it is not eaten. Birds, bats, and small mammals like to eat mantids for a meal.

How They Act

3   Mantids have an interesting way of hunting their meals. They camouflage themselves, changing their body color to match plants and trees near by. This makes them seem like a part of their background. They can sit patiently for a long period of time and look like a branch or leaf. When their meal gets close enough, they strike it down quickly with their front legs. These legs have sharp spines that hold their prey. They move so fast, your eyes would not see how it happened. Most mantids eat the head of their prey first. (For more information about this unusual habit, see http://animals.nationalgeographic.com/animals/bugs/praying-mantis/)

What They Look Like

4   Mantids have five eyes that help them find prey. They have two eyes on either side of their head. They also have three eyes in between the larger eyes. The head of a mantid is shaped like a triangle. It sits on a long thin neck, called a **thorax**. Because a mantid changes colors to go with the background where it lives, it is the most colorful insect in the world. Most adult mantids have wings to fly. Their wings grow on them after they are hatched from eggs. Sadly, mantids live for only about a year.

Fast Facts
- North America has only 20 kinds of mantids, while Africa has 880 species.
- Mantids live in warm or hot areas of the world.
- Most mantids are under six inches in length.

Answer the questions. Mark your answers to questions 4, 6, and 7 on the Answer Form to the right.

Answer Form

4 Ⓐ Ⓑ Ⓒ Ⓓ
6 Ⓐ Ⓑ Ⓒ Ⓓ   **Number**
7 Ⓐ Ⓑ Ⓒ Ⓓ   **Correct** 3

4   Read the following sentences from paragraph 3 of the passage.

> When their meal gets close enough, they strike it down quickly with their front legs. These legs have sharp spines that hold their prey.

What does the word "prey" mean in these sentences?

A an animal that is very similar in size to another animal

B an animal that is caught and eaten by another animal

C an animal that looks like it is praying

D an animal with legs that look like spines

5   Look at the following hyperlink from the end of paragraph 3.

http://animals.nationalgeographic.com/animals/bugs/praying-mantis/

Based on where it is placed in the passage, what kind of information are you **most likely** to find if you follow the hyperlink?

_____

_____

_____

_____

6   Which text feature calls attention to the body parts of a praying mantid?

   A   the key word **"carnivores"**

   B   the key word **"thorax"**

   C   the sidebar

   D   the title

7   Under which heading can you find information about why gardeners like praying mantids?

   A   "What They Eat"

   B   "How They Act"

   C   "What They Look Like"

   D   "Fast Facts"

Performance Task—Extended Response

8 What is the author's point of view on praying mantids? Find **three** examples in the passage that support your answer.

In your answer, be sure to
- tell the author's point of view on praying mantids
- give **three** examples from the passage that show the author's point of view on praying mantids
- use quote marks around words and sentences taken directly from the passage

Check your writing for correct spelling, grammar, capitalization, and punctuation.

Use the space below to plan your essay.

Write your essay on the lines below.

_____

_____

_____

_____

_____

_____

_____

_____

_____

_____

_____

_____

_____

_____

Unit 4
Craft and Structure in Literature

How do you make a castle? You start by building a floor. Next, you put up the walls. You build a few towers. Then you put the roof on top of the walls. You cut out some windows and a door, and you're all set. Each part of the castle is built on the part before it. And all parts are necessary for the castle to be finished. Like building a castle, a writer uses parts to create a story. The writer begins with the first part, or chapter. Then he or she adds more chapters until the book is finished. Each chapter builds on the one before it, and is important to the whole book.

In this unit, you will see how each chapter in a book builds on the chapter that came before, and still adds something new. You'll also learn what poems and plays are made of, and how they are built. Understanding how the parts work together will help you enjoy what you read!

✓ Self Check

Before starting this unit, check off the skills you know below. As you complete each lesson, see how many more you can check off!

I know how to:	Before this unit	After this unit
choose the right meaning of a word based on how it is used in a text.	☐	☐
read chapters of a story to see how they build on each other.	☐	☐
read scenes of a play to see how they build on each other.	☐	☐
read stanzas of a poem to see how they build on each other.	☐	☐
tell the difference between my own point of view and those of the storyteller or the characters.	☐	☐

Lesson 12 Part 1: Introduction 👥

Words in Context

CCSS
RL.3.4: Determine the meaning of words and phrases as they are used in a text, distinguishing literal from nonliteral language.

Theme: *The World Around Us*

Many words have more than one meaning. For example, the word *chill* means "to make cold." But when one person tells another person to "chill," it means "calm down" or "relax." When you read a word or group of words you don't know, you can use nearby words and sentences, or **context clues**, to figure things out.

Read this passage. As you do, think about what *light bulb* means in the passage.

Arthur frowned as he read the directions for putting together his new Phantom Blaster Water Soaker. Then, suddenly, a light bulb lit up in his head. Arthur smiled brightly and said, "Aha! Now I get it!" He quickly snapped together all the parts of his water soaker.

Now, read the passage again. This time, underline any context clues that might help you figure out what *light bulb* means in the passage.

The phrase "a light bulb lit up in his head" doesn't mean that Arthur has an actual glass bulb in his brain. To know the real meaning, you need to use the context clues.

Read the chart below. It shows how to use context clues to find a word's meaning.

Word/Definition	➕ Clues in the Passage	🟰 Meaning in the Passage
Light Bulb: a glass bulb that contains a special wire that produces light when heated.	• A boy frowns while reading directions. • Suddenly, he smiles. • He says, "Aha! Now I get it!"	The word *light bulb* means the boy understands something he didn't understand before—as if a "light" just went on.

Context clues are a reader's friends. You can use them to figure out words you don't know or words with more than one meaning. If you do, light bulbs will go off in your head all the time!

Read the first part of a story about a boy hiking with his family by the ocean.

Genre: **Realistic Fiction**

Seaside Surprises   *by Wendell Riley*

I didn't know what to expect when my family went hiking on the Oregon coast. I'd never seen the Pacific Ocean before. But I sure knew what I wanted to see—a whale!

After a picnic lunch, we hiked through a thick rainforest. We saw chipmunks, a lizard, and a hawk. The trail gently snaked its way up the steep mountainside to the top of a huge rocky cliff with a great view of the ocean. But I couldn't spot any whales. Then we heard something move through the woods right behind us! We turned, and there stood a huge elk with giant antlers.

(continued)

Explore how to answer this question: *"What does the word* snaked *mean as it is used in the story?"*

The word *snaked* describes the trail. It tells how the trail that goes up the mountainside looks.

The chart repeats part of what the writer says about the trail. Write the rest of what he says on the lines provided.

Word/Definition	**+**	Clues in the Passage	**=**	Meaning in the Passage
Snaked: to drag or pull something lengthwise.		"The trail_____ snaked its way up the _____ mountainside to the top of a huge rocky cliff. . . ."		**Snaked:** to move back and forth in a gradual way.

Fill in the blanks to give the meaning of the word *snaked* in the story.

The word *snaked* means to move _____ in a gradual way, rather

than in a _____ line.

Continue reading about the boy's hike by the ocean. Use the Close Reading and the Hint to help you answer the question.

Close Reading

Find and **underline** the animals that the boy still hoped to see, before his eyes "felt locked on the ocean."

(continued from page 122)

Next, the trail wound down to a sandy beach. Waves hammered the shore. We saw seagulls, crabs, clams, and even seals out on the rocks—but no whales. It was fun, but then it was time to go.

Everyone else started walking back to our trail, but my eyes felt locked on the ocean. And then it happened. Not just one whale but a whole pod of them broke the surface of the water. I was so stunned that I could barely shout, "Look!"

Hint

Which choice best describes how the boy looked at the ocean when he saw the whales?

Circle the correct answer.

In the first sentence of the last paragraph, the narrator says that his "eyes felt locked on the ocean." What does the word *locked* mean in this sentence?

A fastened shut

B unable to see well

C unable to look away

D hidden away

✎ **Show Your Thinking**

Look at the answer you chose above. Write two details that helped you understand the meaning of the word *locked* in the story.

_____

_____

_____

 Pick one of the answers you did not choose. Tell your partner why that answer does not tell what *locked* means in the story.

Read the poem. Use the Study Buddy and the Close Reading to guide your reading.

I'm not sure about the meanings of some of the words in this poem. I'm going to circle words I don't know and see if other words in the poem help me figure out their meanings.

Close Reading

What are the leaves doing when they sing songs? **Circle** words that tell what the leaves are doing.

The poet compares the leaves on the ground to people sleeping in their beds. **Underline** the two lines in the poem that describe this.

Genre: **Poetry**

The Wind and the Leaves
by George Cooper

1　"Come, little leaves," said the wind one day,
　　"Come over the meadows with me and play.
　　Put on your dresses of red and gold, —
　　For summer is gone, and the days grow cold."

5　Soon as the leaves heard the wind's loud call,
　　Down they came fluttering one and all.
　　Over the brown fields they danced and flew,
　　Singing the soft little songs they knew.

　　Dancing and whirling, the little leaves went;
10　Winter had called them, and they were content;
　　Soon fast asleep in their earthy beds,
　　The snow laid a coverlet over their heads.

Hints

Reread the first line of the poem. What is the wind calling to come and play?

Use the Hints on this page to help you answer the questions.

1 Read the following line from the poem.

Put on your dresses of red and gold

What is the poet describing in this line?

A leaves changing colors in the fall

B girls getting dressed for a party

C the sky changing colors at sunset

D the wind telling people to dress warmer

Reread lines 5–8. What is causing the leaves to "sing"? How is that sound being made?

2 Explain how the words "singing the soft little songs they knew" describe what the leaves are doing in lines 5–8 of the poem. Use one detail from the poem to support your response.

_____

_____

_____

_____

_____

_____

In the last two lines of the poem, what does the poet say the leaves are doing? How would the fallen snow be like something on a bed?

3 Read the following lines from the poem.

Soon fast asleep in their earthy beds,
The snow laid a coverlet over their heads.

The author uses the word *coverlet* to show that

A the snow looks like a blanket.

B the leaves have fallen.

C the snow looks like a dress.

D the singing has stopped.

Read the story. Then answer the questions that follow.

Yosemite Morning

by Hilary Dumitrescu

1   It is quiet in the park when my brother and I wake up. We pretend we are the only ones here, and not one of thousands of tourists. Fresh snow has fallen overnight and blankets the ground, the rocks, the massive boulders with a silent quilt of white. I take a deep breath. The air smells green and icy. Suddenly, nearby, I hear a soft thump. I hear my brother gasp. When I turn around, he is standing there with his head covered in a thick crown of snow. He laughs and points up. The evergreen branches above him hold armfuls of snow. They are ready to have a snowball fight with us.

2   We walk further into the woods, our boots crunch, crunch, crunching in the snow. My brother walks ahead. At one point, his entire left leg sinks down into the snow. I run to help, and I, too, sink completely into the surprisingly deep snow bank. We are laughing, trying to free our legs from the snow's grip. I pull my foot out, finally, only to find that it's just my sock that has escaped. My boot is still buried. The forest echoes with our giggles, clear as bells.

3   We finally roll, exhausted, away from the deep snow. We continue our exploration. We wander deep into the woods. It feels like we are all alone. I wonder what it must have been for the first people who lived here. What was it like before the cars, the tour buses, the fancy hotels came along? Did they walk, quiet as rabbits, on the new-fallen snow? Did they stare up in awe at the great granite face of Half-Dome?

4   We come to a clearing. My brother holds up a hand, signaling me to stop. At the far edge of the clearing is a small creek, cutting an icy path through the snow. At the creek's edge, a deer is watching us. We freeze. The deer freezes. Slowly, never taking her eyes off of us, she dips her head quickly to the water. She takes a long drink. Her head suddenly shoots up, alerted to sounds only her deer ears can hear. In a flash, she is gone. In the woods, her white tail waves her goodbye.

Half-Dome, Yosemite National Park

5   We decide to head back to our cabin, as the cold air and snowy walk have left us famished. We talk about the breakfast we will have, pancakes with golden butter and syrup. Our parents, we know, will be waiting for us. They have been watching all along, sipping steamy cups of coffee on the porch of our cabin. Later, we will take them into the woods, and show them the silence.

---

1   Read the following sentence from paragraph 1.

> Fresh snow has fallen overnight and blankets the ground, the rocks, the massive boulders with a silent quilt of white.

What does the word "blankets" mean in this sentence?

A   warms

B   covers

C   includes

D   folds up

Answer Form

1 Ⓐ Ⓑ Ⓒ Ⓓ
3 Ⓐ Ⓑ Ⓒ Ⓓ
4 Ⓐ Ⓑ Ⓒ Ⓓ   **Number**
5 Ⓐ Ⓑ Ⓒ Ⓓ   **Correct**   /4

2   Read the following sentence from paragraph 1.

> The air smells green and icy.

Write a paragraph telling what the author shows about the air by calling it "green" and "icy." Use **two** details from the passage to support your answer.

_____

_____

_____

_____

3   Read the following sentence from paragraph 2.

   We are laughing, trying to free our legs from the snow's grip.

   What does the word "grip" mean in this sentence?

   A   to hold or grasp firmly

   B   to have a good understanding

   C   to hold the interest of

   D   to have a sudden pain

4   In paragraph 4, the author writes that the deer "freezes" to show that it

   A   stops quickly

   B   becomes very cold

   C   turns from water to ice

   D   becomes a statue

5   Read the following sentence from paragraph 4.

   In a flash, she is gone.

   The author uses the words "in a flash" to show that the deer ran

   A   through a bright light

   B   in a clumsy way

   C   very quickly

   D   when lightning struck

 **Self Check**   *Go back and see what you can check off on the Self Check on page 119.*

CCSS
RL.3.5: Refers to parts of stories . . . when writing or thinking about a text, using terms such as chapter . . . ; describe how each successive part builds on earlier sections.

Theme: *Learning From Our Choices*

The events that happen in a story are called the **plot**. Most plots present a problem or challenge that the characters try to solve.

Writers often divide longer stories into parts called **chapters**. Each new chapter adds new events and information to the story. Chapter titles can give you clues that tell what happens in each chapter.

Read this table of contents from the chapter book *What They Found on Planet Z*.

Chapter 1: Blast Off to Planet Z

Chapter 2: A Great Mystery Solved

Chapter 3: Telling the World

On the line below, tell what you think happens in Chapter 1.

_____

Now look at the chart below. It shows how what happens in Chapter 3 builds on what happens in Chapter 1 and Chapter 2.

Chapter 1	Chapter 2	Chapter 3
Three astronauts travel in a spaceship to Planet Z.	They solve the mystery of the strange blinking lights on the planet.	When they return to Earth, they tell the world about their discovery.

Good readers think about how each chapter in a book builds on what came before it. When you pay attention to how every chapter adds something new, you have a better understanding of the whole story.

Read the first part of a story about a girl who finds a lost dog.

Genre: **Realistic Fiction**

Keeping the Lost Dog Lost   *by Siri Johnson*

Chapter 1: Finding a Lost Dog

Three weeks ago I found a lost dog on my way home from school. Mom and I couldn't figure out who he belonged to, so we called him "Mystery." It didn't take long before I started hoping that he could stay with us forever. I loved that dog.

Then one night, Mom said, "Jillian, what if we can't find Mystery's owner? Would you like to keep him?" I said, "Yes, yes! Of course!" But then I had a dark thought: *What if we do find the owner?*

(continued)

Explore how to answer this question: *"What problem does Jillian face in Chapter 1?"*

In most stories, the main character must solve some kind of problem. Based on the first chapter of this story, what is Jillian worried about?

Fill in the chart with details from the story that help you understand Jillian's problem.

Events in Chapter 1: Finding a Lost Dog		
Event 1	**Event 2**	**Event 3**
On her way home from school, Jillian finds a lost dog.	Jillian's mom asks her if she would like to keep the _____ if they can't find the _____.	Jillian worries that they will find _____ _____.

Write a paragraph telling what problem Jillian faces in Chapter 1. Use two details from the chart in your answer.

_____

_____

_____

Continue reading about Jillian and the lost dog. Use the Close Reading and the Hint to help you answer the question.

Close Reading

Find and **underline** what Jillian thinks when she first sees the lost dog poster.

(*continued from page 130*)

Chapter 2: Mystery's Real Name

The next day, I was taking Mystery for a walk when I saw a poster tacked to a telephone pole. It had a picture of a lost dog on it. I thought, *Oh no, it can't be!* But there was no question. It was Mystery. Or I should say Barney, because that was his real name. "Are you Barney?" I asked, and he barked three times. Then we walked all over the neighborhood, and I tore down ten more posters. I knew it was wrong, but I couldn't lose . . . Barney.

Hint

What does Jillian do in Chapter 2 that shows what she wants to happen?

Read the question. Then write your answer on the lines.

What happens in Chapter 2 that makes Jillian's problem worse? Use details from the story in your answer.

_____

_____

_____

_____

✎ **Show Your Thinking**

Look at the answer you wrote above. What details from the story helped you describe what made Jillian's problem worse?

_____

_____

 Pick one detail from the chapter that you did not choose. Tell your partner why that detail does not help you explain what made Jillian's problem worse.

Continue reading the story about Jillian and Barney. Use the Study Buddy and the Close Reading to guide your reading.

Genre: **Realistic Fiction**

Chapter 3 starts by telling how Jillian feels about what she did in Chapter 2. I think how she feels will help her solve her problem.

Close Reading

What does Jillian learn from Mrs. Greene about how Barney got lost? **Underline** a sentence that tells what Jillian learns.

What makes Jillian happy? **Circle** the sentence where Mrs. Greene asks for Jillian's help.

Chapter 3: Barney Gets a New Home

1   After I took down all the posters I could find, my happiness disappeared. I knew someone else loved him, and I even knew her name from the poster: Carol Greene.

2   It was wrong to keep a lost dog lost. I knew what I had to do. That night, my Mom said, "Mystery sure seems happy in his new home."

3   "His name is Barney, Mom," I said.

4   "Barney?" she said. "Are you changing his name?"

5   Then I told her the truth. Mom was upset with me at first, but she knew it was all because of how I felt about Barney.

6   Then Mom called the phone number on the poster, and we went to Carol Greene's house. Mrs. Greene ran out of the house the minute we got out of the car. "Barney!" she cried.

7   What Mrs. Greene told us next surprised us. She'd been out of town for a month. She put Barney in a place for dogs, but he escaped. "And he couldn't find me," Mrs. Greene said to me, "so he found you."

8   Mrs. Greene told us she needed to move, and she couldn't take Barney with her. She didn't know what to do before, but she did now.

9   "Jillian," she said. "Could Barney live with you?" She was smiling, but she had tears in her eyes.

10   "I think that would make everyone happy," Mom said.

11   Barney barked and wagged his tail. He agreed.

Hints

Reread paragraph 1. What do you find out about Jillian in this paragraph?

Use the Hints on this page to help you answer the questions.

1 In Chapter 2, Jillian takes down the lost dog posters about Barney because she wants to keep him. How does she feel about her actions at the start of Chapter 3?

   A She feels guilty.

   B She feels relieved.

   C She feels angry.

   D She feels excited.

Where was Mrs. Greene when Barney ran away? Where was Barney at that time?

2 In Chapter 2, Jillian sees the poster. In Chapter 3, she learns Carol Greene's name from the poster. Explain what Jillian learns about Mrs. Greene in Chapter 3 that she did not know before. Use two details from the story to support your answer.

_____

_____

_____

_____

_____

Jillian wanted to do the right thing by telling the truth about the posters. But did she really want to give up Barney?

3 Explain if, by the end of Chapter 3, you think Jillian is happy with her decision to tell the truth about the posters. Use one detail from the story to support your answer.

_____

_____

_____

_____

_____

_____

Read the myth. Then answer the questions that follow.

King Midas and the Golden Touch

a Greek myth

Chapter 1: The King's Wish

1   Long ago there was a king named Midas. Now you might think that a king would have to be wise and thoughtful, but, unfortunately, Midas was a foolish king.

2   Although he was foolish, King Midas was not mean or unkind. He had a daughter whom he loved more than the moon and stars. And Midas himself was much loved by some of the gods who ruled over the ancient world. In fact, one of the gods who loved the king told Midas that he would grant the king anything he wished for.

3   Midas thought this over. If he had thought it over a little bit longer, he might have made a wiser choice. But, besides being foolish, Midas was also a bit greedy. Surely, it was greed that caused Midas to ask for the power to turn everything he touched to gold.

Chapter 2: Midas's Golden Touch

4   Unfortunately for Midas, the god granted his wish. King Midas was overjoyed. He touched the chair he was sitting in, and it turned to gold. He touched the walls of the room, and they turned to gold. He went outside and every plant, flower, and blade of grass he touched immediately changed to the shiny metal. He went to his orchard and pulled an apple from the tree. Midas's golden touch turned the fruit into a glittering ball of gold.

Chapter 3: Too Much of a Good Thing

5   Midas returned to his palace. He called to his servants to bring him food and drink for all this gold-making had made him hungry. The servants brought plates of food to his table. But every bit of food that Midas touched turned to gold before he could get it to his lips. Even the water in his glass turned to a flowing stream of gold as soon as it touched his lips. Midas was beginning to have doubts about his wondrous power, when his beloved daughter came running into the room.

Chapter 4: Washing the Greed Away

6   "Father, father," the young girl cried. "Something terrible has happened in the garden. The soft green grass has turned hard and sharp. And the flowers, father, look at the flowers." She held out two blooms, once living, now cold and hard and golden.

7   Midas reached out to comfort his crying child. As soon as his hand touched her, the girl became a statue of gold, with a golden tear frozen on a golden cheek.

8   "What have I done?" cried Midas. He begged the god who had given him this gift to take it away.

9   The god took pity on Midas. He told the king to go to the nearby river to have his greed washed away. Once he did so, all that the foolish king had once made gold returned to what it had been, including his lovely daughter.

Answer the questions. Mark your answers to questions 1 and 2 on the Answer Form to the right.

Answer Form
1 Ⓐ Ⓑ Ⓒ Ⓓ   **Number**
2 Ⓐ Ⓑ Ⓒ Ⓓ   **Correct**   /2

1   Which sentence from Chapter 1 **best** tells the reader that Midas will likely have trouble with the wish he makes?

    A   "Long ago there was a king named Midas."

    B   "He had a daughter whom he loved more than the moon and stars."

    C   "And Midas himself was much loved by some of the gods who ruled over the ancient world."

    D   "If he had thought it over a little bit longer, he might have made a wiser choice."

2 In which chapter does Midas first begin to see his new power as a problem?

   A Chapter 1: The King's Wish

   B Chapter 2: Midas's Golden Touch

   C Chapter 3: Too Much of a Good Thing

   D Chapter 4: Washing the Greed Away

3 In Chapter 1, Midas is asked to make a wish. In Chapter 2, it is granted. Write a paragraph telling how Midas feels in Chapter 2 about his wish coming true. Use two details from the story to support your answer.

_____

_____

_____

_____

4 Chapter 1 says that Midas "had a daughter whom he loved more than the moon and stars." Write a paragraph telling how Midas shows his love for his daughter in Chapter 4. Use two details from the story to support your answer.

_____

_____

_____

_____

✓ **Self Check** *Go back and see what you can check off on the Self Check on page 119.*

What Are Plays Made Of?

CCSS

RL.3.5: Refer to parts of . . . dramas . . . when writing or speaking about text, using terms such as . . . scene. . . [and] describe how each successive part builds on earlier sections.

Theme: *Adventures, Real and Imagined*

Drama is another word for **play**. A play is a story that actors perform on a stage. Plays are divided into parts called **acts**. Acts may be broken down into smaller parts called **scenes**. Each scene tells one part of the story.

The pictures below are scenes from a play. Think about the story they tell.

Complete the lines below to tell what happens in each scene.

In Scene 1, a family puts things into a _____ .

In Scene 2, the same family _____ .

In Scene 3, that family is resting and playing at _____ .

Now read the chart below. It shows how events and actions build from one scene to the next to tell a complete story.

Scene 1	Scene 2	Scene 3
• The mother and father pack beach chairs and towels into the car. • The children pack sand toys and swim gear.	The family travels in their car with all of their gear loaded in the back.	The family goes to the beach.

Good readers use the parts of a play to help keep track of characters and events. They also think about how one scene leads to the next.

Read the first scene of a play about a spaceship traveling to a distant planet.

Genre: **Drama**

Danger in Deep Space   *by Annika Pedersen*

Scene 1: *The deck of a spaceship. A young pilot, Commander Lyla, is flying the ship. A robot-like figure enters and walks to her side.*

Lyla: *(to robot)* Well, Sam, I sure hope we don't have any trouble getting to Planet Juno. The people there need our help.

Sam: Yes. We must get medicine to them.

(Just then an alarm sounds and a red light flashes over the control panel.)

Lyla: *(looking at controls)* There's someone—or something—in the cargo bay! Come on, Sam. We need to go check it out.

(continued)

Explore how to answer this question: *"What are Lyla and Sam going to do about whatever is in the cargo bay?"*

Look for details in the play that tell what Lyla and Sam plan to do after the alarm sounds.

In the chart below, part of what Lyla says is written under "Event 2" and "Event 3." Write the rest of what she says on the lines provided.

Event 1	Event 2	Event 3
(Just then an alarm sounds and a red light flashes over the control panel.)	Lyla says, "There's _____ _____ in the cargo bay!"	Lyla says, "Come on, Sam. We need to _____ _____ .

Lyla and Sam know something is wrong when the spaceship's alarm sounds and a red light flashes. Lyla can tell that whatever set off the alarm is in the cargo bay of the spaceship.

Fill in the blanks to write about what Lyla and Sam plan to do next.

Lyla and Sam are going to the _____ _____ to find out what is there.

Continue reading about Lyla and Sam's adventure in space. Use the Close Reading and the Hint to help you answer the question.

Close Reading

Lyla and Sam seem to know they are in danger. **Draw a box** around the sentences that tell what happens to them at the end of this scene.

(continued from page 138)

Scene 2: *Lyla and Sam slowly enter the cargo bay of the spaceship.*

Sam: *(to Lyla)* If there's trouble, let's hope our plan works. *(Just then a huge creature enters. It is has an octopus-like head and six arms. It wears a white lab coat.)*

Creature: I am Dr. Blurg from the Planet Mord. I am here to steal your precious supplies. But first, I must put you to sleep. *(Dr. Blurg sprays a green smoke toward Lyla, who falls to the floor. Then he pulls a handful of wires from Sam's back. Sam falls next to Lyla.)*

(continued)

Hint

What does Dr. Blurg want from Sam and Lyla?

Read the question. Then write your answer on the lines.

What happens in Scene 2 that makes the problem on the spaceship worse? Use details from the play to support your answer.

_____

_____

_____

_____

_____

_____

 Show Your Thinking

Pick one detail from the scene that you did not choose. Tell your partner why that detail does not help you understand what made Sam and Lyla's problem worse.

Read the last scene in the play about Lyla and Sam's adventure in space. Use the Study Buddy and the Close Reading to guide your reading.

This part of the play tells why Dr. Blurg is doing what he's doing. I'll pay attention to why Blurg is acting like he is.

Close Reading

How did Sam and Lyla know that Dr. Blurg might try to steal from them? **Underline** a sentence that tells you how they knew.

Dr. Blurg says that he plans to take the medicine to his planet. **Circle** a sentence that shows why he needs the medicine.

(continued from page 139)

Scene 3: *Back on the deck of the spaceship. Dr. Blurg is at the spaceship's controls, all six arms working at once.*

Dr. Blurg: My plan is working perfectly! I'll dump Lyla and her helpless robot on some safe planet. Then I will return to my planet with the medicine. I'll be a hero! *(Sam enters. Then, Lyla appears and makes an impossible leap through the air and lands next to Dr. Blurg.)*

Sam: I think there's been a change of plans, Dr. Blurg.

Dr. Blurg: But this is impossible! *(He looks to Lyla.)* My secret sleeping gas should put you to sleep for at least 24 Earth hours! *(Dr. Blurg sprays Lyla again with the green gas. She fakes a yawn, then she jumps ten feet in the air, lands, and shrugs.)*

Dr. Blurg: And you, robot. I cut your power supply! How. . . .

Sam: Things are not what they seem, Dr. Blurg. *(Sam takes off his "head," which is more like a space helmet.)* You see, you've got things backwards. I'm the human. And Lyla, she's the most amazing "machine" in space.

Dr. Blurg: Why, she's hardly more than a girl! I'll take care of her. *(He goes after Lyla, who grabs Dr. Blurg and lifts him over her head with one hand. Dr. Blurg shouts.)* You tricked me!

Sam: Our secret agents on your planet told us that you might try something like this. We were ready for you.

Dr. Blurg: But my poor planet! We won't survive without your special medicine.

Sam: If you're willing to make peace, we will get medicine to your people. Now let's take this ship to your Planet Mord.

(Lyla sets Dr. Blurg down and gently brushes him off.)

Hints

Why didn't Dr. Blurg's green gas work on Lyla? Why didn't pulling out Sam's wires stop Sam?

Use the Hints on this page to help you answer the questions.

1 Scene 2 ends with Lyla and Sam falling to the floor of the cargo bay. Explain how Scene 3 tells what really happened. Use two details from the play to support your answer.

_____

_____

_____

_____

_____

Who told Sam and Lyla that Dr. Blurg might try something?

2 In Scene 2, Sam says to Lyla that he hopes their "plan" works. Write a paragraph about what we learn in Scene 3 that explains why they made a plan to fool Dr. Blurg. Use one detail from the play to support your answer.

_____

_____

_____

_____

_____

Do Lyla and Sam want to help Dr. Blurg, even after what he tried to do to them?

3 In Scene 3, Lyla and Sam find out why Dr. Blurg wants to steal the medicine. Explain what this leads them to do. Use one detail from the play to support your answer.

_____

_____

_____

_____

_____

Read the play. Then answer the questions that follow.

from *How the Animals Got Their Beautiful Coats*

from a play based on a Zulu folktale, retold by Pat Betteley

Characters: Storyteller, Tortoise, Leopard, Zebra, and Hyena

Act 1, Scene 1

Storyteller: Sakubona, visitors. Welcome to our village. Sit down by the fire, and I will tell you a story. You all know that Zulus are very careful about their looks.

Even the animals in this land are well groomed. But this was not always so. In the beginning, all animals in Africa were a dull brown color. Hyena was not only drab but also mean. He liked to play tricks on smaller animals. One day he knotted a piece of vine around one of Tortoise's feet and hung him from a high branch. Then Hyena ran away, laughing.

Tortoise: Help, someone! Please, help me!

Leopard: Calm down, little one. I'll help you.

Tortoise: Mr. Leopard, please hurry. I don't want to die!

Storyteller: Leopard quickly lowered Tortoise and untied him.

Tortoise: Thank you, friend Leopard. You could have made a meal of me, but instead you saved my life. Please let me do something for you in return.

Leopard: (*chuckling*) What can a little tortoise like you do for a big leopard like me?

Tortoise: I can make you beautiful.

Leopard: (*smiling*) Very well. I accept your offer.

Act 1, Scene 2

Storyteller: Tortoise mixed a silver-yellow color from the petals of flowers and painted Leopard's coat.

Zebra: My, my, that is the most handsome coat in the forest. Where did you get it?

Leopard: My friend, Mr. Tortoise, made it for me.

Zebra: I must find him. Maybe he'll make one for me as well.

Storyteller: Zebra hurried down the path until he came upon Tortoise.

Zebra: Oh, Mr. Tortoise, Mr. Leopard's coat is so handsome. Please paint my coat, too.

Storyteller: Tortoise painted black and white stripes all over Zebra's coat. He finished up by painting Zebra's dainty hoofs a glossy black.

Zebra: Thank you, Tortoise. These stripes will be perfect for hiding in the tall grass.

Act 1, Scene 3

Storyteller: Zebra went along down the path. Soon he met Hyena.

Hyena: (*sneering*) Hey, where'd you get that coat?

Zebra: From my friend, Mr. Tortoise. Do you like it?

Hyena: I'd never wear it, but it fits you, I suppose. Where's Tortoise?

Storyteller: Zebra pointed down the path, and Hyena loped off to find Tortoise.

Hyena: (*in a threatening voice*) I want a beautiful coat, too. Give me one or I'll hang you from the tree again.

Tortoise: (*looking him over carefully*) H-m-m-m. I think I see just what will be best for your size and shape.

Storyteller: So Tortoise mixed many colors together in one pot and smeared them all over Hyena's coat. When Hyena slunk away, it was a good thing he could not see himself, for he was all blotched, with a dirty white, gloomy gray, and dull brown coat. And he is still that way today—the messiest-looking animal in Africa—labeled clearly as a mean and unpleasant character!

1 What event in Scene 1 causes all the other events in the play to happen?

Answer Form

1 Ⓐ Ⓑ Ⓒ Ⓓ **Number** / 2
2 Ⓐ Ⓑ Ⓒ Ⓓ **Correct**

   A A storyteller invites listeners to sit by a fire.

   B Hyena hangs Tortoise from a high branch.

   C Leopard shows his handsome new coat to Zebra.

   D Tortoise paints black and white stripes on Zebra.

2 In Scene 1, Tortoise tells Leopard that he can make him beautiful. Which line in Scene 2 **best** shows that Tortoise was telling the truth?

   A "My, my, that is the most handsome coat in the forest."

   B "My friend, Mr. Tortoise, made it for me."

   C "Zebra hurried down the path until he came upon Tortoise."

   D "Tortoise painted black and white stripes all over Zebra's coat."

3 Tell why Hyena wants to find Tortoise in Scene 3. Use one detail from the play in your answer.

_____

_____

4 Tell why Tortoise paints Hyena with a dull, blotchy coat in Scene 3. Use one detail from the play in your answer.

_____

_____

✓ **Self Check** *Go back and see what you can check off on the Self Check on page 119.*

Lesson 15   Part 1: Introduction 👥

What Are Poems Made Of?

CCSS

RL.3.5: Refer to parts of . . . poems when writing or speaking about a text, using terms such as . . . stanza . . . . [and] describe how each successive part builds on earlier sections.

Theme: *Poems That Tell a Story*

Many poems tell stories. But poems usually look different from stories. Most poems are written in short **lines**. When the lines are grouped together, the group of lines is called a **stanza**. Like the chapters in a story, the main ideas in stanzas build on each other.

Read the poem below.

A Penguin's Life

I'm a bird that has two little wings,
but they do not make me fly.
The air above is not for me.
The ocean is my "sky."

In icy seas, I swoop and soar,
a swimmer fast and bold.
You'd swim fast, too, if you were me
because that water sure is cold!

Read the poem again. Draw a box around each stanza. Number them "1" and "2."

The poem has two stanzas. The stanzas work together to present an idea about a penguin. But what is that idea?

The chart below shows how the stanzas work together to make an idea. Complete the chart.

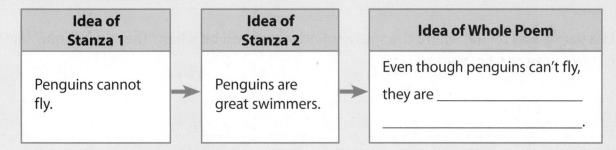

Idea of Stanza 1	Idea of Stanza 2	Idea of Whole Poem
Penguins cannot fly.	Penguins are great swimmers.	Even though penguins can't fly, they are _____ _____.

Good readers look at how the lines in a poem are organized into stanzas. When you learn to see how a poem is built, you will better understand how the ideas in stanzas build on each other.

Read two stanzas of a poem about a puppy.

Genre: **Free Verse**

Little Puppy　*from the Navajo*

Little puppy with the black spots,
Come and herd the flock with me.
We will climb the red rocks
And from the top we'll see
The tall cliffs, the straight cliffs,
Where the eagles live.

We'll see the dark rocks,
The smooth rocks,
That hold the rain to give us
Water, when we eat our bread and meat,
When the sun is high.

Explore how to answer this question: *"Where will the speaker and the puppy be when the sun is high?"*

In this poem, the speaker tells the puppy where they will go and what they will do. The second stanza tells more things they will see and do in that place.

Look for details in the poem that explain what the speaker tells the puppy they will do. Then fill in the missing words in the chart below.

What Happens in Stanza 1?	What Happens in Stanza 2?
When they herd a flock of animals, the speaker tells the puppy they will _____ to the top of the red _____ .	The speaker tells the puppy they will see different types of _____ , and they will eat _____ when "the sun is high" (the middle of the day).

Write a paragraph telling where the speaker and puppy will be when "the sun is high." Use details from the chart in your paragraph.

_____

_____

_____

_____

Read the following poem. Use the Close Reading and the Hint to help you complete the activity that follows.

Genre: **Limerick**

Old Man with a Beard

from A Book of Nonsense *by Edward Lear*

There was an Old Man with a beard,
Who said, "It is just as I feared!—
⠀⠀⠀Two Owls and a Hen,
⠀⠀⠀Four Larks and a Wren,
Have all built their nests in my beard."

Close Reading

Each line of the poem adds something. **Circle** the line that tells who the poem is about.

Hint

Go back and read each line. Figure out what each line adds to the poem.

Complete each sentence. Then answer the question.

The first line of the poem tells that the poem is about _____.

The second line of the poem shows that the man has a _____.

The third and fourth lines of the poem list _____.

Tell how the last line builds on the other lines of the poem.

_____

_____

_____

✎ **Show Your Thinking**

"Old Man with a Beard" is a type of poem called a *limerick*. Limericks are often meant to be funny. Which line makes this poem funny? Explain your answer.

_____

_____

_____

 With a partner, discuss how all of the lines work together to make the poem into a joke.

Read the poem. Use the Study Buddy and the Close Reading to guide your reading.

This poem has three stanzas. I'm going to write a few words about the main idea of each stanza. This will help me understand the story the poem is telling.

Close Reading

How does the acorn start to change in the second stanza? **Circle** words that tell you what it looks like.

What does the acorn turn into in the third stanza? **Underline** words that tell you what it has become.

Genre: **Narrative Poem**

Little by Little   *Anonymous*

"Little by little," an acorn said,
As it slowly sank in its mossy bed,
"I am improving every day,
Hidden deep in the earth away."

Little by little, each day it grew;
Little by little, it sipped the dew;
Downward it sent out a thread-like root;
Up in the air sprung a tiny shoot.

Day after day, and year after year,
Little by little the leaves appear;
And the slender branches spread far and wide,
Till the mighty oak is the forest's pride.

Hints

How does the acorn start to change after it sinks underground?

Use the Hints on this page to help you answer the questions.

1 The poem "Little by Little" tells a story about an acorn in three stanzas. Explain what happens to the acorn in stanza 1. Use two details from the poem to support your answer.

_____

_____

_____

_____

_____

What happens to seeds when they are in the ground for a while?

2 Write a paragraph that summarizes what happens to the acorn in stanza 2. Use two details from the poem to support your answer.

_____

_____

_____

_____

_____

Each stanza of the poem tells about a step in how something grows. What has happened to the acorn by the end of the poem?

3 Explain what happens to the acorn in stanza 3. Use two details from the poem to support your answer.

_____

_____

_____

_____

_____

149

Read the narrative poem. Then answer the questions that follow.

The Truth About the Dragon's Tooth

by John Hansen

1　The king called me to his throne
　　and said, "That dragon must be slayed!"
　　I bowed and played the brave, strong knight,
　　but in truth . . . I was afraid.

2　As I dressed in shining armor
　　and sharpened sword and lance,
　　a voice inside me whispered,
　　"You haven't got a chance!"

3　I climbed upon my faithful horse
　　and rode off into the gloom.
　　I hoped I'd see my home again
　　on the other side of doom.

4　I rode into the mountains
　　and faced the dangerous beast.
　　The dragon licked its lips and said,
　　"A man, a horse—a feast."

5　I raised my lance to charge it,
　　thinking, What else can I do?
　　Then the trees behind it crashed and fell
　　as a giant marched in view!

6　The earth beneath began to shake,
　　his huge figure blocked the sun.
　　Then the giant shouted happily,
　　"Why, I've found you, little one!"

7　As he bent down to catch the dragon,
　　I began to understand:
　　The dragon was the giant's pet,
　　scooped up in one huge hand.

8 The giant turned to me and said,
 "Your people will want proof
 that you bravely faced my dragon,
 so I'll give you this baby tooth."

9 He reached into the dragon's mouth
 and wiggled out a monster fang,
 then tossed it through the air at me.
 It hit my shield—clang!

10 The people cheered when I returned
 and waved the dragon's sword-like tooth.
 But I found I was afraid again—
 Afraid to tell the truth!

---

1 Read these lines from stanza 3 of the poem.

 I hoped I'd see my home again
 on the other side of doom.

Explain why the knight worries about ever seeing his home again.
Use **two** details from the poem to support your answer.

_____

_____

_____

_____

_____

_____

2 Stanza 6 begins, "The earth beneath began to shake." What happens in stanza 5 that explains why this happens?

Answer Form

2 Ⓐ Ⓑ Ⓒ Ⓓ   **Number**   /2
4 Ⓐ Ⓑ Ⓒ Ⓓ   **Correct**

   A   The dragon attacks the knight and his horse.

   B   The knight charges the dragon with his lance.

   C   A giant marches toward the knight and dragon.

   D   Some trees are cut down in the forest nearby.

3 Describe what happens in stanza 7 that explains why the giant has appeared. Use **one** detail from the poem to support your answer.

_____

_____

_____

_____

_____

4 Why does the giant toss the dragon's tooth at the knight in stanza 9?

   A   He wants the knight to leave the dragon alone.

   B   He is afraid of the brave knight and tries to scare him.

   C   He hopes the knight will tell people that he has a pet dragon.

   D   He wants to give the knight proof to show he faced the dragon.

✓ **Self Check**   *Go back and see what you can check off on the Self Check on page 119.*

Point of View

CCSS
RL.3.6: Distinguish their own point of view from that of the narrator or those of the characters.

Theme: *Making Friends*

In stories, characters can look at events in different ways. Each character has a **point of view,** or a way of thinking and feeling about what is happening. The person telling the story (the **narrator**), the characters, and even the readers all have points of view.

Look at each person in the cartoon below. Think about each person's point of view.

It's my new delicious recipe for green bean ice cream!

Now, write a word by each person that tells how each one feels about the ice cream.

How did each person feel? Did they all feel the same way? No. They all had different points of view about the ice cream. You probably have your own point of view, too.

Read the chart below. In the last column, tell your own point of view about green bean ice cream.

Different Points of View on Green Bean Ice Cream			
How the Girl Acts	**How the Boy Acts**	**How the Man Acts**	**How Would You Act?**
Delighted	Disgusted	Proud	_____ _____

When you read a story, think about all of the different points of view in it. This will help you understand who is telling the story and how the characters feel about events.

Read the first part of a story about an owl and a bat.

Genre: **Modern Fantasy**

Night-Flying Friends   *by Sean Vincent*

Last night, I sat perched on a branch in a tall oak tree, seeing everything with my big owl eyes. Some crazy creature flew this way and that through the air. What was his problem? Then he landed—upside down!—on the tree trunk next to me. He was a young brown bat. He talked a mile a minute about all the bugs he'd just eaten and a thousand other things. Just before he left, he said, "My name's Max! Good talking with you." Had I said a word?

"Mine is Alec," I hooted.

(continued)

Explore how to answer this question: *"What is the owl's point of view on the bat the first night they meet?"*

The owl is telling the story. He is also a character in the story. Look for details that tell what the bat does and what the owl thinks about that.

Part of what the bat does is listed below. On the lines provided, fill in the rest of what the bat does and what the owl thinks about it.

What the Bat Does	What the Owl Thinks
"Some _____ creature flew this way and that through the air."	"What was his _____?"
"He talked _____ about all the bugs he'd just eaten and a _____ other things."	"Had I said _____?"

Write a paragraph telling the owl's point of view about the bat on the first night they meet. Use details from the chart in your response.

_____

_____

_____

Continue reading about Max and Alec. Use the Close Reading and the Hint to help you answer the question.

Close Reading

Why does Alec hope Max will come back on the second night? **Underline** sentences that tell why he wants to see Max again.

(continued from page 154)

The next night, I kept hoping Max would come back. True, his strange ways troubled me. He eats mosquitoes and flies in a wild way. But we are both creatures of the night, and we can both fly. And it would be good to have someone to talk with. When I finally saw him, I swooped through the air. "Hey, Max," I said, "Want to stop by my place after dinner?" He said he'd like that. We talked, and then we flew through the night together, our first flight as friends.

Hint

Does Alec see any ways in which he and Max are alike?

Circle the correct answer.

How does Alec's point of view on Max change on the second night they meet?

A He sees that Max could teach him a lot about flying.

B He is less sure than before that he could be friends with Max.

C He thinks Max is too strange to be any kind of a friend.

D He sees that he and Max have enough in common to be good friends.

✎ Show Your Thinking

Look at the answer you chose above. What were the details that helped you understand how Alec's point of view changed on the second night?

_____

_____

_____

 What is your point of view on the way Max acts? Tell your partner why you have this point of view. Use details from the story to support your response.

Read the story. Use the Study Buddy and the Close Reading to guide your reading.

Genre: **Fiction**

The narrator doesn't seem to be a character in the story. I know this because the narrator tells the story but isn't a part of the action.

Close Reading

Why does Sam like talking with the prince? **Underline** sentences that tell why he enjoys being with the prince.

What happens when Sam speaks to Prince Oliver? **Circle** sentences that show how the prince reacts to Sam.

The Stable Boy and the Prince
by John Martinsson

1   Sam offered the apple he'd found to the horse, Shadowfax. He stroked the horse's huge head and wished for a moment that Shadowfax could talk. Six months had passed since Sam had been taken from his village to work at the king's stables, and it had been a very lonely time for him.

2   Just then, the prince came riding past. Prince Oliver was about the only other boy his age that Sam ever saw. As the prince passed, Sam knelt and bowed his head. But as he looked down, he saw a huge snake coiling up in the prince's path. The prince's horse reared back and then bolted.

3   With hardly a thought, Sam jumped on Shadowfax and raced after Prince Oliver, who was struggling to stay in the saddle. But no horse was faster than Shadowfax. Sam reached the prince and grabbed his horse's reins.

4   The prince thanked Sam for his efforts. As they rode back to the castle, the prince spoke pleasantly with Sam. When they reached the stables, Sam said, "I hope we can talk again. It's so good to speak with someone my own age."

5   The prince fell silent. Then he said, "Remember your place. I am a prince, and you are just a stable boy."

6   Sam bowed and returned to the barn. "I'll never have a friend here," he whispered. Shadowfax walked over and rubbed his face against him. Sam hugged the horse. "What am I saying, my friend?" he said. "I've got you."

Hints

Reread paragraph 1. What do you learn about Sam in this paragraph?

Would Sam like to be friends with the prince? How does the prince speak to Sam, at first?

What does Prince Oliver say to Sam when Sam speaks to him?

Use the Hints on this page to help you answer the questions.

1 What is Sam's point of view on working at the king's stables?

  A   He is excited because he can ride Shadowfax.

  B   He is lonely because he has no friends.

  C   He feels lucky to have such an important job.

  D   He is bored because he has only a horse to talk with.

2 Write a paragraph telling about Sam's point of view on Prince Oliver in paragraph 4. Use two details from the paragraph to support your answer.

_____

_____

_____

_____

_____

_____

_____

_____

3 What is Prince Oliver's point of view on Sam?

  A   He would like to be friends with the boy who rescued him.

  B   He thinks it would be fun to race horses with Sam.

  C   He thinks it is wrong for him to be friends with a stable boy.

  D   He feels sad that he is too old to be friends with Sam.

Read the story. Then answer the questions that follow.

Basketball Ballet

by Lori Anastasia, Highlights

"There's a new kid in our class," I told my friend Aidan as we hung up our coats at the back of the classroom.

"How do you know?" Aidan asked.

"He moved in next door to me," I said, sitting down at my desk. "Mom and I brought muffins over yesterday."

"Class, please welcome Brady Walker," Ms. Simpson said. My new neighbor stood beside her.

"Brady, tell the class something about yourself," Ms. Simpson said.

"I'm from California," said Brady. "I have a dog that eats all my stuff."

Everyone giggled. His dog sounds just like mine, I thought.

"I like baseball and basketball. And I take dance class."

"Dance class," Aidan yelled. "That's for girls!"

The whole class laughed. Brady's face turned bright red.

"That's enough," Ms. Simpson said.

At lunch, Brady walked over to an empty seat at my table.

"Hi, Emilio," Brady said to me. "Thanks again for those awesome muffins. Can I sit here?"

I was about to say yes, but Jordan put his foot on the chair. "This seat is taken," he said. "Sit with the girls."

Aidan laughed.

Brady walked away and sat by himself.

That afternoon, Brady sat by himself on the bus. I felt bad for him. I thought about sitting with him, but I didn't want to get picked on.

I remembered how everyone teased me when I knit a scarf for Ms. Simpson. I didn't like being teased, so I gave up knitting. But what would have happened if I'd stood up for myself?

When I got home, I made a peanut butter and pickle sandwich. My dog, Gus, was barking by the living-room window. I walked over to see why. Brady was shooting baskets in his driveway. He was really good!

I went back into the kitchen to get my sandwich, but it was gone. Gus stood by the counter with a tiny pickle hanging from his mouth.

The next day, we had gym with Coach Kelley.

"Today we're playing basketball," Coach Kelley announced. "Emilio and Natalie will be captains. Emilio, you pick first."

I looked around the room and noticed Brady. It felt like giant robots were wrestling inside my stomach. I didn't want to get laughed at. But I knew what I had to do.

"I choose Brady," I said.

"What?" Aidan yelled. "He can't play basketball."

A giant smile spread across Brady's face. He ran up and stood beside me.

"Why did you pick me?" he asked.

"I wasn't a good friend yesterday," I said. "Plus, I know you're good at basketball."

We started playing. Brady made 10 baskets and stole the ball from Aidan four times.

"Wow," Aidan said to Brady. "Where did you learn those moves?"

Brady smiled. "Ballet class."

Aidan looked at me, then at Brady. "Could you teach me?"

Brady, Aidan, and I started hanging out together all the time after that. Usually, we were in Brady's driveway, practicing our basketball ballet.

Answer the questions. Mark your answers to questions 1–3 on the Answer Form to the right.

Answer Form

1 Ⓐ Ⓑ Ⓒ Ⓓ
2 Ⓐ Ⓑ Ⓒ Ⓓ   **Number**
3 Ⓐ Ⓑ Ⓒ Ⓓ   **Correct** /3

1 What is Aidan's point of view on the new student, Brady, in the first part of the story?

   A He thinks Brady is an interesting new classmate.

   B He thinks Brady is a stranger who needs his help.

   C He thinks Brady is a person to be made fun of.

   D He thinks Brady is someone he'd like to be friends with.

2 How does Aidan's point of view on Brady change by the end of the story?

   A He thinks Brady is silly to enjoy ballet.

   B He admires Brady and becomes his friend.

   C He worries that Brady will start dancing on the basketball court.

   D He thinks that Brady won't teach him his basketball moves.

3 Why is it hard for Emilio to choose Brady for his basketball team?

   A He fears that Aidan and others will laugh at him for choosing Brady.

   B He has an upset stomach and doesn't want anyone else to know.

   C He is the only one who knows that Brady is good at basketball.

   D He worries that Brady might want to become friends with him.

4 Explain what your point of view on Brady is. State whether it is more like Emilio's or Aidan's. Use **one** detail from the story to support your answer.

_____

_____

_____

_____

_____

_____

✓ **Self Check** *Go back and see what you can check off on the Self Check on page 119.*

Read the poem. Then answer the questions that follow.

Squirrel

by Mary Ann Hoberman, A Little Book of Little Beasts

1   Grey squirrel
          Small beast
      Storing up a winter's feast,
      Hides a hundred nuts at least.

2   Nook and cranny stocked with seed
      Tucked away for winter's need.
      Acorns stuck in hole and crack.
      Will he ever get them back?

3   When the snow is piled up high
      And the year is at December,
      Can he really still remember
      Where he hid them in September?

4   I have watched him from my window
      And he always seems to know
      Where the food he hid is waiting
      Buried deep beneath the snow.

5   And I wonder
          (Do you wonder?)
      How he knows where he must go.

1   Answer Parts A and B below.

Part A

What is one main idea of "Squirrel"?

A   A person carefully watches a squirrel through the window.

B   A squirrel prepares for winter by hiding nuts and seeds.

C   It is amazing that squirrels can find all the food they have hidden.

D   Squirrels may not remember all the places they must look for food.

Part B

Which lines from the poem **best** support the answer to Part A?

A   "And he always seems to know / Where the food he hid is waiting"

B   "Can he really still remember / Where he hid them in September?"

C   "Nook and cranny stocked with seed / Tucked away for winter's need."

D   "Acorns stuck in hole and crack. / Will he ever get them back?"

2   Read the following lines from stanza 2 of the poem.

> Nook and cranny stocked with seed
> Tucked away for winter's need.

The author uses the words "Tucked away" to show that

A   the seeds are warm in the nooks and crannies

B   the seeds will fall off the tree into the winter snow

C   the seeds are safely put away, to eat in the winter

D   the seeds will grow in the nooks and crannies

3 Read the following lines from stanza 3 of the poem.

> Can he really still remember
> Where he hid them in September?

Which words in stanza 4 answer this question?

A "watched him from my window"

B "he always seems to know"

C "the food he hid"

D "Buried deep"

4 Read the last stanza of the poem.

> And I wonder
>   (Do you wonder?)
> How he knows where he must go.

Based on the stanzas that come before this last stanza, what is the speaker wondering about? Use **two** details from the poem to support your answer.

_____

_____

_____

5 Which **best** describes the speaker's point of view on the squirrel?

A She thinks the squirrel is clever.

B She thinks the squirrel is annoying.

C She thinks the squirrel is silly.

D She thinks the squirrel is selfish.

Read the play. Then answer the questions that follow.

Campfire Songs

by Bernie Paw

Characters
BEAR
RACCOON
BOBCAT

Act I, Scene 1

(Three animals—a raccoon, a bear, and a bobcat are walking through the forest looking for something to do.)

BEAR: Well, now that we've all had our dinner, what are we going to do for fun? (*He looks bored, walking slowly with head down*)

RACCOON: I've had all the nuts I need for a week. What else is there to do around here? (*He kicks a stone and sends it flying*)

BOBCAT: I'm full of meat! It sure is a boring night in the forest.

RACCOON: Hey, what's happening over there in the clearing? (*He looks curious, his whiskers shaking*) Ah, some humans. They're sitting around a fire. It might be fun to watch them and see what they do. Humans can do some strange things!

BOBCAT: (*Shaking her head and smiling*) What are they eating? (*She looks through some bushes*) What kind of food is that? (She *laughs*)

Act I, Scene 2

(The campsite is growing darker except for a campfire that is burning brightly like a candle. The animals are hidden behind some large bushes, watching with interest.)

BEAR: (*Staring through bushes, scratching his head*) Well, look at that, what are those weird puffy little white squares the boy is putting on a stick into the fire? Why do you suppose they would do that?

RACCOON: I don't know. Why are they using little odd-shaped sticks with five pointy ends to eat their food? Why don't they just use their paws like us? (*He makes a disgusted face at the people.*)

BEAR: Well, if that don't beat all! The man is putting his fresh fish over the fire on some kind of a flat rock. Why do you suppose they need to burn perfectly fresh fish on a fire? (*He seems confused, shaking his head side to side*)

BOBCAT: (*Rolls her eyes*) Look at the meat, it's on top of the fire and they're burning that, too! (*She laughs crazily, rolling on the ground holding her sides*)

Act I, Scene 3

(*The animals continue to watch the humans and then see another odd thing in the camp.*)

BEAR: (*Lays down on his belly and pushes more bushes out of his way*) Look, look there! What's that funny box the woman is holding in her hands with strings? Can you hear those sounds she is making when she touches it?

The campers start to sing along with the guitar music. At first, bear, bobcat, and raccoon look startled. Their eyes are opened wide, big as saucers. They continue to listen to the music and singing. As they listen, they begin to smile.

RACCOON: Hmm. This is starting to sound kind of nice. Almost as pretty as Owl's hoot and Wolf's howl.

(*The animals lean on each other, eyes closed, and begin to slowly sway back and forth to the music. All three begin to yawn.*)

BOBCAT: (*Sleepily*) Well, humans sure are strange, but they can make the sweetest sounds.

BEAR: (*Almost asleep, but still swaying to the music*) Hm. Hmm.

RACCOON: And here we thought there would be nothing interesting to do tonight.

(*One by one, Bear, Bobcat, and Raccoon curl up next to each other and fall asleep to the music.*)

6 Read the following sentence from Scene 3 of the play.

> Their eyes are opened wide, big as saucers.

The author uses the words "big as saucers" to show that

A the animals are very tired

B the animals are very surprised

C the animals can't see in the dark

D the animals' eyes look round and hard

7 In Scene 1, the animals think it will be fun to watch the humans because "humans can do some strange things." In Scene 2, what do the animals discover about humans that they think is strange? Use **two** details from the play to support your answer.

_____

_____

_____

_____

8 What is the animals' point of view on the humans by the end of the play?

A They think that the humans are too silly.

B They think that the humans are too noisy.

C They think that the humans are funny, but also frightening.

D They think that the humans are strange, but also interesting.

Performance Task—Extended Response

9 At the beginning of the play, the animals feel bored. However, their feelings change during the play. Tell how the animals feel in Scene 1, Scene 2, and Scene 3 to show how their feelings change. Use at least **three** details from the play to support your answer.

In your answer, be sure to
- tell how the animals feel in Scene 1, Scene 2, and Scene 3
- explain why their feelings change during the play
- use **three** details from the play to support your answer

Check your writing for correct spelling, grammar, capitalization, and punctuation.

Use the space below to plan your essay.

Write your essay on the lines below.

_____

_____

_____

_____

_____

_____

_____

_____

_____

_____

_____

_____

_____

_____

How is a good reader like a wise shopper? A wise shopper wants to see the real item. The words that describe it are just not enough. Here's an example—you want to buy a backpack. You want to see it, feel it, and try it on. Reading the words on the tag isn't good enough. Good readers look at the pictures when they read. The pictures help them understand what they learn from the words. A wise shopper wants to compare items. One backpack might feel better than another. Or the price might be better. Good readers want to compare, too. They compare two passages in order to get more information about a topic.

In this unit, you'll learn to use maps and photographs to help you understand what you read in a passage. You will also read and compare two passages about the same topic. You'll see how they are alike and different. By doing this, you'll get more information about the topic.

✓ Self Check

Before starting this unit, check off the skills you know below. As you complete each lesson, see how many more you can check off!

I know how to:	Before this unit	After this unit
use the maps in a text to help me understand the passage.	☐	☐
use the pictures in a text to help me understand the passage.	☐	☐
describe the way sentences and paragraphs use cause and effect and sequence.	☐	☐
describe the way sentences and paragraphs compare ideas.	☐	☐
compare and contrast the most important ideas in two texts on the same topic.	☐	☐

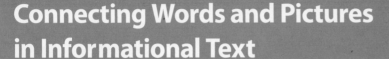
Connecting Words and Pictures in Informational Text

CCSS

RI.3.7: Use information gained from illustrations (e.g., maps, photographs) and the words in a text to demonstrate understanding of the text (e.g., where, when, why, and how key events occur).

Theme: *Looking at Inventions*

Many texts include pictures that can help you better understand the information in a passage. **Maps** are drawings of places, and they show where things are located. **Photographs** and **illustrations** show what something looks like.

Look at the map and read about Pleasant Lake.

At Pleasant Lake you can enjoy boating, fishing, water skiing, and swimming. The lake is located 15 minutes from Mt. George. Campsites are available. Call 111-1212 now!

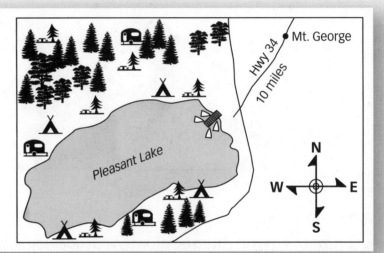

On the map, draw the direction you must go to get from Mt. George to Pleasant Lake.

The text gives you some information about Pleasant Lake. The map gives you other information about it. If you combine the information from the text and the map, you get a complete picture. The chart below shows this.

What the Text Tells	What the Map Shows
• what you can do at Pleasant Lake • how long it takes to get to Pleasant Lake from Mt. George • the number to call for campsites	• how far it is to Pleasant Lake • the roads you take to Pleasant Lake • where Pleasant Lake is located • where the campsites are located

Always look at the pictures that come with a passage. Maps, photographs, and illustrations are meant to help you better understand the topic of a passage.

Read the first part of an advertisement for a new invention from Japan.

Genre: **Advertisement**

The Invention That Dogs Are Barking About!

Do you know what your dog is saying when it barks? Now you can find out. A company in Japan has invented a tool that can tell you! The newly invented gadget senses your dog's bark, then sends the information to a handheld device. This device shows you if your dog is happy, sad, excited, or scared. Order this amazing invention today. Your dog will thank you!

(continued)

Explore how to answer this question: *"What does the illustration help you understand about the device?"*

Look for key details in the text. Then look closely at the illustration. How does the device work?

Complete the chart below by adding a detail from the illustration that is not described in the text.

What the Text Tells	What the Illustration Shows
• The device was invented in Japan. • It shows what a dog is feeling. • It sends information to a handheld device.	• A picture shows up on the handheld device. • One part of the device is placed around the _____.

Fill in the blanks below to tell what the illustration helps you understand about the device.

The illustration shows that the device fits _____ a dog's neck. A picture appears

on a screen that shows you what the dog is _____ when it barks.

Continue reading about the invention from Japan. Use the Close Reading and the Hint to help you answer the question.

Close Reading

On the map, **draw a circle** around Japan. Then **circle** the United States.

(continued from page 172)

Although at first the device was only sold in Japan, it's now available in the United States.

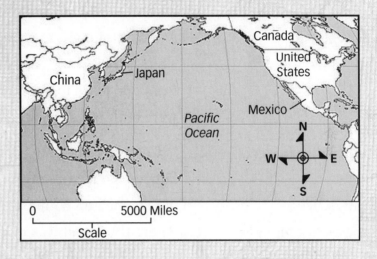

Hint

Use the compass to help you answer the question. In a compass, "E" stands for "East; "W" stands for "West; "N" stands for "North"; and "S" stands for "South."

Circle the correct answer.

The text tells you that, at first, the invention was only available in Japan. According to the map, which direction do you need to go to travel from the United States to Japan?

A East

B West

C North

D South

✎ **Show Your Thinking**

Look at the answer that you chose above. Explain why your answer is correct.

_____

_____

 With a partner, use the mileage scale on the map to find about how many miles are between the western coast of the United States and Japan.

Read the history passage. Use the Study Buddy and Close Reading to guide your reading.

Genre: **History**

After I read the passage, I'll look at the map. It will help me understand why the author thinks canals are one of the greatest inventions.

Close Reading

How is the old route different from the route through the Panama Canal? **Circle** the number of miles that tell the distance for each route.

What information tells you why canals are important? **Underline** two details in the text that explain why canals are important.

The Amazing Canal *by Dell Sutclif*

1   Right up there with the wheel, the road, and the steam engine, the canal is one of the greatest inventions in the world. A canal is a passageway for water. It creates a shortcut to allow people and goods to travel easily by boat from one place to another. Some of the first canals for travel were built in Egypt nearly 4,000 years ago.

2   Completed in 1914, the Panama Canal is one of the most famous modern canals. It cuts 51 miles across the Isthmus of Panama and connects the Atlantic and Pacific Oceans. Before the Canal was built, ships had to go around the tip of South America. The Canal made the trip much shorter, faster, and safer.

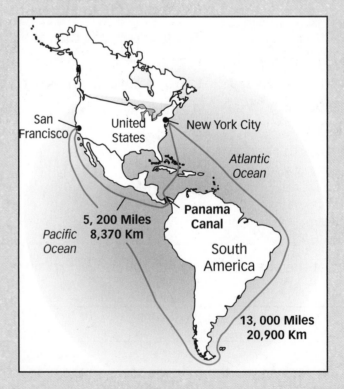

Hints

Look back at the map. What is on each side of the canal?

Use the Hints on this page to help you answer the questions.

1 According to the map and the text of the passage, what does the Panama Canal connect?

   A The Atlantic Ocean and the Pacific Ocean

   B North America and South America

   C Egypt and the United States

   D New York City and the tip of South America

How do canals help people?

2 Based on the map and the text, what does the map show you about canals?

   A After the Panama Canal was built, most people still wanted to travel around the tip of South America.

   B The Panama Canal created a shorter but no less dangerous route.

   C The Panama Canal helps people and goods get from one place to another more easily.

   D Canals were widely used in ancient times, but are not in use today.

Which details in the passage and the map show that the canal is a great invention? Put these details together to support your answer.

3 The author says that the canal is one of the greatest inventions. Write a paragraph telling why the canal is one of the greatest inventions. Use one detail from the passage and one detail from the map to support your answer.

_____

_____

_____

_____

_____

_____

Read the passage. Then answer the questions that follow.

Riiip! Thanks, George!

by Hannah Ford

1   Riiip! That familiar sound is what we might hear when we undo our shoes or open our backpacks. It's Velcro! One side is fuzzy. The other side is prickly. It sort of feels like . . . a prickly plant? Well, that's because a prickly plant was the inspiration for Velcro.

2   George Mestral, the man who invented Velcro, lived in a country in Europe called Switzerland. One day, he was hiking in the Jura Mountains near his home. When he came home, he found lots of sticky burrs on his pants and socks. *What makes these stick?* he wondered. He decided to look at them under a microscope.

A burr

3   Close up, George saw that each little spine on the burr ended in a hook. When he looked at the fibers of his pants and socks, he noticed they were little loops. The hooks from the burrs got caught on the little loops. That got George thinking. *These things have real sticking power. Imagine if they could stick things together in a useful way!*

4   After many years of experimenting, George was able to re-create the sticking power of the little burrs. He made two pieces of fabric: one piece that was covered in prickly hooks, the other that was covered in soft, fuzzy loops (see Figures A and B). Put them together and they hung on tight! With a hearty tug, riiip! They came apart!

5   George was eager to share his invention. A lot of people told him it was silly. George knew better. He knew that his invention could take the place of many fasteners. Zippers, buttons, pins, and shoelaces would all become a thing of the past, he claimed. In 1951, he patented his invention. He named it "Velcro," a combination of the words *velour* ("velvet") and *crotchet* ("hook"). He began manufacturing it, sure that it would have thousands of uses. He was right.

Figure A

Figure B

6   Velcro's first big fan was NASA. Astronauts had lots of bulky equipment to put on and take off. Velcro proved to be a strong, easy-to-pull-off fastener for spacesuits. It could hold tools in place so they wouldn't float away. Skiers also wore bulky suits. They liked how Velcro fasteners held tight and opened easily. Sneaker makers saw Velcro straps as kid-friendly. Even toddlers could fasten and unfasten their straps!

7   From something most people find annoying, George Mestral gave us a wonderful convenience. The next time you hear that riiip, thank him!

Answer the questions. Mark your answers to questions 1, 2, and 4 on the Answer Form to the right.

Answer Form

1 Ⓐ Ⓑ Ⓒ Ⓓ
2 Ⓐ Ⓑ Ⓒ Ⓓ **Number** /3
4 Ⓐ Ⓑ Ⓒ Ⓓ **Correct**

1 Which sentence from the passage **best** explains how George Mestral got the idea to invent what is shown in Figure B?

  A "Close up, George saw that each little spine on the burr ended in a hook."

  B "When he looked at the fibers of his pants and socks, he noticed they were little loops."

  C "He named it "Velcro," a combination of the words *velour* (velvet) and *crotchet* (hook)."

  D "Even toddlers could fasten and unfasten their straps!"

2   According to the photographs and the text of the passage, how is the photograph of a burr on page 176 like the photograph in Figure A?

   A   Both grow on a plant.

   B   Both are brownish in color.

   C   Both have tiny hooks on the ends.

   D   Both are shaped like tiny insects.

3   George Mestral made two different kinds of fabric. Write a paragraph telling what made those kinds of fabric stick together. Use **two** details from the passage and the photographs to support your answer.

_____

_____

_____

_____

_____

_____

4   What is a reason that astronauts first started to use Velcro?

   A   It held tools in place so they wouldn't float away.

   B   It allowed astronauts to wear sneakers.

   C   It allowed astronauts to walk inside a spaceship.

   D   It helped astronauts walk safely on the moon.

✓ **Self Check**   *Go back and see what you can check off on the Self Check on page 169.*

Lesson 18   Part 1: Introduction 👥

Making Connections Between Sentences and Paragraphs

CCSS

RI.3.8: Describe the logical connection between particular sentences and paragraphs in a text (e.g., . . . cause/effect, first/second/third in a sequence).

Theme: *Food Inventions*

One way writers connect ideas is to tell about what happened and why it happened. Sentences use signal words such as *because, so, as a result*, and *since* to connect a **cause,** or reason, to its **effect** (what happened).

Writers also connect sentences and paragraphs by showing how things happen in **sequence**, or order. Look for signal words in sentences such as *first, then*, and *finally* to see how ideas and events are connected by the order in which they happen.

Read the paragraph below about the invention of the sandwich.

> Who ate the first sandwich? John Montague, the Fourth Earl of Sandwich, of course! Because the Earl of Sandwich was very busy one day, he didn't have time for a fancy meal. So he asked his cook to make something that would be easy to eat. First, the clever cook sliced some meat. Then, he cut two slices of bread. Finally, he put the meat between the slices of bread. As a result, the sandwich was born!

Now read the paragraph again. As you read, circle three cause-and-effect signal words and underline three sequence words.

Read the chart below. It shows how the ideas in the paragraph are connected.

Why It Happened (Cause)	What Happened (Effect)	Order It Happened (Sequence)
"Because the Earl of Sandwich was very busy one day, he didn't have time for a fancy meal."	• "So he asked his cook to make something that would be easy to eat." • The cook put meat between two slices of bread and "the sandwich was born!"	1. The Earl of Sandwich was busy. 2. He asked his cook for something easy to eat. 3. The cook created a sandwich.

When you read, look for how the ideas in sentences and paragraphs are connected. Looking for signal words will help you understand the relationships between ideas.

Read the first two paragraphs of a science passage about the food people eat in space.

Genre: **Science**

Space Food   *by Claire Daniels*

Astronaut food has changed over the years. In the early days of space exploration, astronauts traveled in small spacecraft, where there was little room for food. Fresh foods in early space travel were not practical. They spoiled, took up too much space, and were too heavy.

As a result, astronauts in space ate freeze-dried foods. Freeze-dried foods don't spoil. They don't weigh much, and they don't take up much space. Add water and you have "fresh" peas, mashed potatoes, steak, or macaroni and cheese. There is even freeze-dried ice cream!

(continued)

Explore how to answer this question: *"How are the two paragraphs in this passage connected?"*

What is the most important idea in each paragraph? Think about the main thing you learn in each paragraph. Circle signal words to help you see how the paragraphs are connected.

Read the chart below. It shows the relationship between the most important ideas in the paragraphs.

Why It Happened (Cause)	What Happened (Effect)
"Fresh foods in early space travel were not practical."	"As a result, astronauts in space ate freeze-dried foods."

Fill in the blanks below to write about how the two paragraphs are connected.

Paragraph 1 tells the cause, or why astronauts didn't eat _____

in space. Paragraph 2 tells the effect, or what happened as a result: Astronauts ate

_____ . The paragraphs are connected by _____

and effect.

Continue reading about space food. Use the Close Reading and the Hint to help you answer the question

Close Reading

How are the sentences connected? **Underline** signal words that show sequence, or the order in which things happen.

(continued from page 180)

Foods are freeze-dried in a food plant. First, vegetables and fruits are washed and cut up. Foods like meats and pasta are cooked. Second, the food is frozen to −40 degrees Fahrenheit. Then, workers grind the food into smaller pieces or into a powder. Finally, the foods are dried to remove 98 percent of the water.

Today, astronauts travel with freezers and ovens, so they don't depend on freeze-dried foods. Still, many people who go on backpacking and boat trips often use them.

Hint

Which signal word that you underlined gives a clue about the third step in the process?

Circle the correct answer.

Which sentence tells the third step in freeze-drying foods?

A "First, vegetables and fruits are washed and cut up."

B "Foods like meats and pasta are cooked."

C "Then, workers grind the food into smaller pieces or into a powder."

D "Finally, the foods are dried to remove 98 percent of the water."

✎ Show Your Thinking

Look at the answer that you chose above. Explain why you chose the answer by listing the steps that come before and after it.

_____

_____

_____

 Describe to your partner how you do something (such as how you get ready for school). Use signal words such as *first, next, then*, and *finally* to list details in the order they happen.

Read the feature article. Use the Study Buddy and Close Reading to guide your reading.

I wonder why people eat such "weird" foods. I'll look for causes and underline them.

Close Reading

How is hakarl made? In paragraph 3, **circle** a signal word that shows the order of the steps.

Why did American pioneers eat crickets and other bugs? **Underline** the words that tell why.

from "Freaky Foods"

by Nancy Shepherdson, Boy's Life

1   Around the world, including America, people enjoy what others might call "weird" foods. Snakes, bats, bugs, camel's hump. Think about that the next time your mom fixes you spinach or broccoli or liver. Wouldn't you rather have roasted termites instead?

Fish for Breakfast

2   In Japan, many kids eat fish first thing in the morning. Makes sense, in a country surrounded by water. Later in the day, they might have jellyfish. The sting from these jellyfish can kill, so the poison must be removed first. That takes four to eight days of soaking in cold water. After that, all that's left is a crunchy treat, like chicken nuggets, usually eaten with a dipping sauce.

3   Other fishy meals around the world include fermented shark, or hakarl, eaten in Iceland. To make hakarl, just bury a shark in sand for three years, then dig it up and dig in.

You're Bugging Me!

4   Ounce for ounce, insects are a great source of energy. When food supplies ran low, American pioneers ate Mormon crickets and other bugs on the journey West. In more than half the world today, including Africa, Australia, Europe, Asia and America, insects are on the menu.

Hints

What kind of connection do the words *first* and *later* show?

Use the Hints on this page to help you answer the questions.

1 Read these two sentences from paragraph 2.

> In Japan, many kids eat fish first thing in the morning.

> Later in the day, they might have jellyfish.

Which of the following describes the relationship between these two sentences?

A The sentences describe steps in a process.

B The second sentence tells the cause of the event described in the first sentence.

C The first sentence tells the cause of the event described in the second sentence.

D The sentences describe the order of two events.

Write the steps in the order they need to happen. Use words like *first, next,* and *then.*

2 State the steps taken to prepare hakarl. Write the steps in order.

_____

_____

_____

_____

Sentences don't always use signal words to make connections. But you can still find the connections they make by looking at each part of the sentence. For example, ask yourself: "Why did American pioneers eat insects?"

3 Read this sentence from the last paragraph.

> When food supplies ran low, American pioneers ate Mormon crickets and other bugs on the journey West.

How are the ideas in this sentence connected?

A The sentence shows steps in a process.

B The sentence compares two events.

C The first part of the sentence tells the reason for the event described by the second part.

D The second part of the sentence tells the cause of the event described by the first part.

Read the feature article. Then answer the questions that follow.

Patriotic Pizza

by Karin Gaspartich, Highlights

1   Two thousand years ago, Greeks baked flat disks of bread and used the bread like a plate. They would first eat the food on top of the bread. Then they would eat the bread "plate."

2   People started to put toppings on the flat bread before it went into the oven. This was an early form of today's pizza.

3   In Italy, many centuries later, people also ate a form of pizza. It was considered food for the poor. Most people had flour, water, oil, and spices. They could use these ingredients to make a simple pizza.

4   Working-class people of Naples had short breaks for meals. They needed cheap food that could be eaten quickly. Pizza made by local vendors was a perfect solution. It could even be eaten without plates and forks.

A Queen's Favorite Pizza

5   In 1889, Queen Margherita and King Umberto I of Italy took a vacation in the seaside town of Naples, Italy. The queen saw people strolling outside eating pizza. She wanted to try some pizza for herself.

6   Raffaele Esposito was a popular pizza maker in town. He was chosen to make a pizza for the queen. Esposito wanted his pizza to be extra special. So he made a pizza using the colors of the Italian flag: red, green, and white. Red tomatoes, green basil (an herb), and white mozzarella cheese went on his patriotic pizza.

7   Esposito baked his creation, and it was delivered to the queen. She loved it. She sent a note of praise and thanks. Raffaele named it Pizza Margherita in honor of the queen. Soon everyone wanted to try it.

8   Around that time, workers began leaving Italy to live in America. Pizza bakers brought their talent and recipes with them. Gennaro Lombardi opened the first pizzeria in New York City in 1895. Early pizzerias had no chairs. People just went in, ordered their pizza, and left with it.

9   Pizza became popular with American workers, too. It was tasty and easy to eat on the go. Before long, pizza was one of the most popular foods in the United States.

10   Perhaps you could invent your very own pizza. Have fun . . . And finish your plate!

Make a mini Margherita pizza!

Ask an adult to help you with this recipe.

You will need:

- 3 English muffins
- 1 tomato, sliced
- 10 fresh basil leaves, cut in half
- 3/4 cup of shredded mozzarella cheese
- toaster oven (or conventional oven)

1. With an adult's help, preheat the oven to 350 degrees Fahrenheit.

2. Split the English muffins with a fork. On each half, put some mozzarella cheese, a slice of tomato, and a few pieces of basil.

3. Place the mini pizzas on a tray, and ask an adult to put them in the oven. Cook the pizzas for 10 minutes or until the cheese is melted.

4. Ask an adult to take your mini pizzas out of the oven. Share them.

Answer the questions. Mark your answers to questions 1–3 on the Answer Form to the right.

Answer Form

1 Ⓐ Ⓑ Ⓒ Ⓓ
2 Ⓐ Ⓑ Ⓒ Ⓓ   **Number** ╱3
3 Ⓐ Ⓑ Ⓒ Ⓓ   **Correct**

1 Read these two sentences from paragraph 6.

Esposito wanted his pizza to be extra special.

So he made a pizza using the colors of the Italian flag: red, green, and white.

Which of the following describes the relationship between these two sentences?

A The first sentence explains the reason for the second.

B The sentences compare pizza to the Italian flag.

C The second sentence gives the cause of the first.

D The sentences describe the steps to make a Margherita pizza.

2 Reread paragraphs 5 and 6. Which question about the events in paragraph 6 is answered in paragraph 5?

  A Who was Queen Margherita?

  B Why did Esposito make a pizza for the queen?

  C What are the colors of the Italian flag?

  D What did Esposito name his special pizza?

3 Paragraph 9 tells that pizza become popular in the United States. How does paragraph 8 explain why this happened?

  A It tells that Italian pizza bakers coming to America brought their recipes for pizza with them.

  B It explains that the first pizza places in the United States did not have chairs, so people stood while eating.

  C It tells that most people could afford flour, oil, and spices to make their own pizzas.

  D It describes how the pizza crust could be used like a plate.

4 State the order of the directions you need to follow in step 2 of the recipe for a mini Margherita pizza. Use **three** details from the passage to support your answer.

_____

_____

_____

_____

_____

✓ **Self Check** *Go back and see what you can check off on the Self Check on page 169.*

Describing Comparisons

CCSS

RI.3.8: Describe the logical connection between particular sentences and paragraphs in a text (e.g., comparison . . .).

Theme: *Ancient Inventions*

Sentences and paragraphs can be connected by **comparing** facts and ideas. Writers compare things to show how they are alike or different. Signal words such as *however, but, different,* and *unlike* are used to describe differences. Signal words such as *like, as, also,* and *both* are used to show how things are alike. Sentences and paragraphs use these words to make **comparisons**.

Read the following paragraph.

> Like people today, ancient peoples wanted to keep their teeth clean. They also used toothbrushes. However, their brushes were very different. Our toothbrushes are plastic with nylon bristles. But the first toothbrushes were made of twigs with crushed ends.

Now read the paragraph again. This time, circle any signal words being used to make comparisons.

Read the chart below to see how specific sentences compare ideas.

Sentences	Signal Words	Comparisons
"Like people today, ancient peoples wanted to keep their teeth clean."	The word "Like" signals that the sentence tells how two things are **alike**.	The sentence shows how two things are **alike** by stating that both ancient peoples and people today want to keep their teeth clean.
• "However, their brushes were very different." • "Our toothbrushes are plastic with nylon bristles." • "But the first toothbrushes were made of twigs with crushed ends."	The words "However" and "But" signal that these sentences tell how two things are **different**.	The sentences show how two things are **different** by describing the differences between toothbrushes today and toothbrushes in ancient times.

Good readers notice how sentences and paragraphs are connected by comparisons. This will help you understand how ideas and events in a text are alike or different.

Read the first two paragraphs of a passage about toothpaste.

Genre: **Social Studies**

Ancient Toothpaste   *by Tom Wiggins*

1   People like to have clean, white teeth. Today, we can just pick up a tube of toothpaste, squeeze it, and brush our teeth with the paste. Today's toothpaste is made from sodium fluoride (which keeps our teeth strong), a whitener, and flavoring.

2   The first tooth cleaner was made in Egypt over 1,600 years ago. Like today's tooth cleaners, it was a paste. However, ancient toothpaste was made differently. It contained mint, dried iris flower, rock salt, and pepper grains. Today we use toothbrushes to apply our toothpaste, but the Egyptians rubbed the paste on their teeth with a finger.

(continued)

Explore how to answer this question: *"How are the two paragraphs in this passage connected by a comparison?"*

What is the most important idea in each paragraph? What signal words connect these ideas?

Fill in the blanks in the chart to show how the paragraphs are connected.

Sentences	Signal Words	Comparison
• "Today's toothpaste is made from sodium fluoride (which keeps our teeth strong), a whitener, and flavoring." • "However, ancient toothpaste was made differently."	• "However" • "differently"	Paragraph _____ tells what _____ toothpaste is made from. Paragraph _____ tells what _____ toothpaste was made from.

Fill in the blanks to write about how the two paragraphs are connected by a comparison.

The two paragraphs are connected by a comparison because the _____ paragraph

describes modern toothpaste and the _____ paragraph shows how ancient

toothpaste is _____ from modern toothpaste.

Continue reading about toothpaste. Use the Close Reading and the Hint to help you answer the question.

Close Reading

Reread the last sentence of each paragraph. What do they tell you about the difference between modern and ancient toothpastes? **Circle** the word "However" in the last sentence.

(continued from page 188)

The ancient toothpaste in Egypt came in one flavor: mint. Today, our toothpaste comes in many flavors. We can choose from mint, cherry, and even bubblegum! Using toothpaste is fun and makes our teeth feel good.

Even with the minty taste, ancient toothpaste tasted unpleasant and strong. Like our toothpaste, it did clean the teeth. However, ancient toothpaste was not fun to use— it was painful on the gums and made them bleed.

Hint

In what kind of comparison is the signal word "however" used?

Circle the correct answer.

How are the two paragraphs in this passage connected?

A They compare by describing how modern toothpaste and ancient toothpaste are different.

B They compare by describing that ancient toothpaste tasted bad because it was too strong.

C They compare by telling that both modern and ancient toothpastes came in different flavors.

D They compare by telling that both modern and ancient toothpastes were fun to use.

✎ **Show Your Thinking**

Look at the answer that you chose above. Choose one answer you did not choose and tell why it is incorrect.

_____

_____

 Using at least two signal words, tell your partner how two things you know about are alike or different.

Read the social studies passage. Use the Study Buddy and Close Reading to guide your reading.

Genre: **Social Studies**

The writer tells about the Inca Road by comparing it to the longest Roman road. I'm going to underline ways that these two roads were alike or different.

Close Reading

How were the Romans and Incas different? **Underline** sentences that tell about their differences.

How are modern suspension bridges different from the Incas' suspension bridges? **Draw boxes** around the sentences that tell how they were different.

The Great Inca Road   *by Hilary Dumitrescu*

1   Roads are difficult to construct and expensive to maintain. However, a great civilization needs great roads. Roads connect people to the goods they need to live. They allow the government to send help when it is needed. Even the most ancient civilizations understood the need for good roads.

2   High in the Andes mountains, the Incan Empire thrived for centuries. When the Spanish first explored the Andes in the 16th century, they were amazed by the roads they found. Even the longest Roman road, the Via Appia, was not as long as the Incas' Royal Way. It was 3,500 miles long. Like the Via Appia, the Royal Way connected the capital to other parts of the empire. More roads connected to it. All in all, the Inca road system, known as the Inca Road, stretched for 23,000 miles.

3   Unlike the Romans, the Incas did not have wheels or carts. Instead, they rode llamas. These sturdy pack animals carried people and goods all over the empire. Messengers known as *chasquis* ran along the Inca Road carrying messages from the king to all parts of the empire.

4   The Inca Road passed through high mountains. To safely cross the deep mountain ravines, the Incas built amazing suspension bridges. These bridges were not made out of steel like modern suspension bridges. Instead, they were woven out of plant fibers! But the Spanish found that the bridges were strong enough to carry soldiers and horses safely.

Hints

Reread paragraph 2. What signal words show how the Via Appia and The Royal Way roads were alike?

Reread each answer choice. What signal words show how two things are different?

What two materials for building bridges do these sentences tell about?

Use the Hints on this page to help you answer the questions.

1 Which sentence from paragraph 2 tells how the two roads described in the passage were alike?

A "When the Spanish first explored the Andes in the 16th century, they were amazed by the roads they found."

B "Even the longest Roman road, the Via Appia, was not as long as the Incas' Royal Way."

C "Like the Via Appia, the Royal Way connected the capital to other parts of the empire."

D "All in all, the Inca road system, known as the Inca Road, stretched for 23,000 miles."

2 Which sentence from the passage best tells a way that the Romans and the Incas were different?

A "Roads connect people to the goods they need to live."

B "High in the Andes mountains, the Incan Empire thrived for centuries."

C "Unlike the Romans, the Incas did not have wheels or carts."

D "These sturdy pack animals carried people and goods all over the empire."

3 Read these sentences from paragraph 4.

These bridges were not made out of steel like modern suspension bridges. Instead, they were woven out of plant fibers!

Identify the two things being compared in these sentences. Write the signal words in the sentences and tell what kind of comparison they make.

_____

_____

_____

_____

Read the article. Then answer the questions that follow.

from "Writing On a Wasp's Nest"

by Kacey Hartung, Appleseeds

1   You're outside on a warm spring day. You hear a buzzing sound over your head. On a nearby tree branch, you see a nest shaped like an upside-down umbrella. Wasps! Are you scared, or do you try to get a better look? Now think about this: A nest like that one led to the invention of something you would have a hard time living without—paper!

A wasp's nest

2   Before paper was invented, the ancient Chinese wrote on pieces of silk cloth. But silk was expensive. The empress (or queen) of China wanted something to write on that would be cheaper and easier to make than silk. So she asked a palace worker named T'sai Lun to find a new material to write on. This happened about 1,900 years ago.

3   According to the story, T'sai Lun remembered seeing an empty wasp's nest as a boy. The nest was made of a strong, lightweight material. T'sai Lun knew that if he could create a material like the wasp's nest, he would solve the empress's problem.

4   The job wasn't easy. It took T'sai Lun three years to come up with the perfect mixture: tree bark, scraps of fishing nets, and water. He boiled and beat the mixture into mush. Today we call the mush "pulp." Then he stretched a piece of cloth across a wooden frame and dipped it into the pulp. When he lifted the frame, a thin layer of pulp remained on top of the cloth. After drying in the sun, the layer formed kog-dz, which means "paper made from bark of mulberry tree."

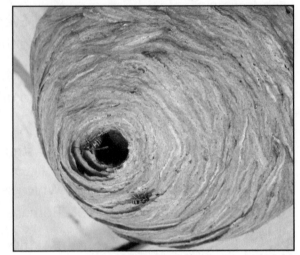

Ancient Chinese writing

5   The Chinese were proud of T'sai Lun's invention and tried to keep the recipe for kog-dz a secret. Slowly, traders from China brought kog-dz to Japan, northern Africa, and Europe. As the use of kog-dz spread, the ingredients changed. In Europe, the people used cloth rags

instead of tree bark. The rags worked well, but there were not enough to make all the paper that people wanted.

6   Today, paper is still made in the same basic way that T'sai Lun made it thousands of years ago. Wood is cut into small pieces, then broken down into pulp by large grinding machines. The pulp is sprayed onto a wire screen and heated until the paper is dry.

7   We make different papers for different uses: soft tissue, stiff cardboard, colorful construction paper, smooth paper for computers, and glossy paper for magazines. They look and feel different, but they are all made from wood.

8   Would you have thought that a wasp's nest could lead to a product we use every day? Before you run from those wasps, thank them for sharing their "recipe" for paper and changing our lives. Then you can run—after all, you don't want to get stung!

Answer the questions. Mark your answers to questions 1, 2, and 4 on the Answer Form to the right.

Answer Form

1 Ⓐ Ⓑ Ⓒ Ⓓ
2 Ⓐ Ⓑ Ⓒ Ⓓ   **Number**
4 Ⓐ Ⓑ Ⓒ Ⓓ   **Correct** /3

---

1   As described in paragraph 5, how was papermaking in Europe different from papermaking in China?

    A In Europe, there were more rags available than tree bark.

    B In Europe, paper was made from a wasp's nest instead of tree bark.

    C In Europe, paper was made from cloth rags instead of tree bark.

    D In Europe, the rags worked much better than tree bark.

2   What two things are compared in paragraph 6?

    A how modern papermaking and ancient papermaking are alike

    B the different ways that wood is cut into pieces during papermaking

    C the different types of grinding machines used to make pulp

    D how modern wire screens and ancient wire screens are different

3 Read the following sentence from paragraph 7.

> They look and feel different, but they are all made from wood.

State what is being compared in this sentence. Use **two** details from the passage to support your response.

_____

_____

_____

_____

_____

_____

4 Read this sentence from paragraph 3.

> T'sai Lun knew that if he could create a material like the wasp's nest, he would solve the empress's problem.

How is paper like the wasp's nest that T'sai Lun saw?

A Both are made from tree bark.

B Both are glossy and smooth.

C Both are stiff and colorful.

D Both are lightweight and strong.

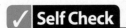 **Self Check** *Go back and see what you can check off on the Self Check on page 169.*

Lesson 20 Part 1: Introduction 👥

Comparing and Contrasting Two Texts

CCSS

RI.3.9: Compare and contrast the most important points and key details presented in two texts on the same topic.

Theme: *Inventions That Changed the Way We Live*

Imagine you are reading two texts about the same topic. Even though the topic is the same, the texts are not identical. You can **compare** the main ideas and details in those texts, or tell how they are alike. You can also **contrast** them, or tell how they are different. Let's look at two texts about one of the most famous machines in history.

Read the ad and the news story.

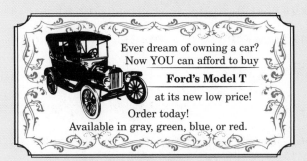

Ever dream of owning a car? Now YOU can afford to buy

Ford's Model T

at its new low price!

Order today!
Available in gray, green, blue, or red.

A Car For Everyone
October, 1908

Today Henry Ford rolled out his newest car, the Model T. The lower price of this car, nicknamed the "Tin Lizzie," makes it affordable for everyone.

Circle the details in the ad and news story that are alike. Underline the details that are different.

Look at the diagram to see how to compare and contrast the ad and the news story about the Model T Ford.

Model T Ad	**Both**	**Model T News Story**
• shows what the Model T looks like • comes in gray, green, blue, or red	• affordable	• nicknamed "Tin Lizzie" • made by Henry Ford • went on sale in October, 1908

The main ideas of the ad and news story are alike: The Model T is affordable. The key details are different: The ad has a picture and tells that the Model T comes in different colors. The news story tells about the Model T's nickname, who made the car, and when it became available.

When reading two texts on the same topic, compare and contrast the main ideas and details to see how they are alike and different. It's a skill of good readers everywhere.

Read this passage about the history of computers.

Genre: **History**

A Short History of Computers   *by Spencer Kay*

In 1833, a man named Charles Babbage came up with the idea of the modern computer. But there was one problem. He couldn't figure out how to make one.

A hundred years later, things changed. In 1939, the first computers were invented to help countries fight wars. Then, from 1950 on, companies used computers to help run their businesses. These computers were so huge that they filled large rooms.

In 1981, the first PC, or personal computer, was sold. It fit on a desktop and had a keyboard and a screen. Since then, computers have become faster, smarter, and smaller. Today, you can even hold a computer in your hand!

Explore how to answer this question: *"What is the main idea of this passage?"*

What are the key details in each paragraph? How do these details help you determine the main idea of the passage?

Read the chart to see how the key details in the passage can help you find the main idea.

Paragraph 1	Paragraph 2	Paragraph 3
In 1833, Charles Babbage introduced the idea of a modern computer, but he didn't know how to make it.	• In 1939, the first computers helped countries fight wars. • In 1950, companies began using huge computers.	• In 1981, the first PC was sold. • Since the early 1980s, "computers have become faster, smarter, and smaller."

What do the details tell about what has happened to computers over time?

Fill in the blanks below to write about the main idea of the passage.

The passage tells how the modern _____ has _____ since it was first invented.

Now read a passage about how we use computers today. Use the Close Reading and the Hint to help you answer the question.

Close Reading

In the first paragraph, **underline** the sentence that tells the main idea of the passage. Then **circle** two key details in the second paragraph that support the main idea.

Genre: **Social Studies**

Computers Today   *by Spencer Kay*

Fifty years ago, few people knew much about computers. Even thirty years ago, not many people had them. But today computers are everywhere!

You might be surprised to learn how many computers you use every day. Digital watches and cameras use computers. So do TVs and cell phones. Cars and airplanes use them. They are also in traffic lights, alarm clocks, and MP3 players.

Hint

Choose an answer that tells about the main ideas, not just the details in the passages.

Circle the correct answer.

How are the main ideas of "A Short History of Computers" and "Computers Today" different?

A The first passage tells how computers have changed. The second tells how we use computers every day.

B The first passage tells about computers used in wars. The second tells about computers used in cars.

C The first passage tells who invented the computer. The second tells why computers were invented.

D The first passage tells how companies use computers. The second tells how cameras use computers.

Show Your Thinking

Look at the answer that you chose above. Explain why your answer tells the main ideas of the passages, not just a detail from each.

_____

_____

"Computers Today" states, "Even thirty years ago, not many people had them." With a partner, find a detail in "A Short History of Computers" that supports this idea.

Read these two passages about television. Use the Study Buddies and Close Reading to guide your reading.

Genre: **History**

To get ready to compare and contrast the two passages, I'm going to look for the key details in this first passage to find its main idea.

Close Reading

How popular did television become in the United States? **Circle** sentences that tell how many U.S. households had televisions by 1946 and how many had them in 1962.

Based on the title and the key details, what is this passage mostly about? **Underline** details that support the main idea.

History of Television   *by Marcus Fink*

1   David Sarnoff had an idea. If sound could travel over the radio, why couldn't pictures? In 1939, he showed the world it was possible. Broadcast television was born.

2   No one person can claim that he or she invented television. People in several countries were inventing it about the same time. But even though television was invented, there was a catch. No one knew what to do with it. Sarnoff did, and he knew where to introduce it.

3   In 1939, Sarnoff showed the first television broadcast at the New York World's Fair. People crowded around the tiny sets to watch the black-and-white pictures. The first show was of President Franklin D. Roosevelt, who gave a speech. That same year, television sets went on sale. The first ones were small—only 5-inch by 12-inch screens.

4   Television companies began showing programs. In 1939, the first baseball game was put on television. Stations began to broadcast news shows, children's shows, comedies, and dramas. Today there are hundreds of channels and many more kinds of programs.

5   In 1946, there were about 6,000 televisions sets in use in the United States. In 1951, there were 12 million. As more people watched, more shows were added. By 1962, around 49 million U.S. households had televisions in the home. Today, 99 percent of homes have a television. Some even have three or more!

I'm going to look for key details in this passage. Then I'm going to draw lines between the ideas in both passages that are alike.

Close Reading

What opinions about watching television does the author state? **Circle** two opinions in the passage.

How does the passage answer the question asked by the title "Should We Watch TV?" **Underline** two details that help answer this question.

Genre: **Persuasive Essay**

Should We Watch TV? *by Zak Shimek*

1   What do you do in your free time? If you say, "watch television," you are not alone. About 99 percent of American households own a television. The airwaves are flooded with all kinds of programs. There are hundreds of channels to choose from.

2   And there's so much to see! You can watch a tiger hunt in the jungle—something you might never see in person. You can visit the bottom of the ocean or cruise in outer space from your sofa. You can learn how to do new things, such as cook. TV is also a good way to relax. Watching a funny show can be relaxing.

3   But do Americans watch too much television? One study said that the average person watches four hours each day. If that person lived to be 65 years old, he or she would have watched TV for nine years!

4   Watching television doesn't require effort. All you have to do is sit and watch. When children watch TV, they are not playing and running. They aren't playing games or solving problems. Also, children who watch a lot of TV tend to eat more junk food including chips and soda. So watching a lot of TV can be bad for your health.

5   Watching a little television each day isn't harmful. It might even make you smarter. But if you are watching four hours a day, think about doing something else!

Hints

Which answer choice is found in both passages?

Use the Hints on this page to help you answer the questions.

1 Which of the following is a key detail found in both passages?

- **A** Watching television might make you smarter.
- **B** Too many Americans watch too much television.
- **C** The first television screens were only 5 inches by 12 inches.
- **D** Most households in America have a television.

Which sentence from "Should We Watch TV?" does not support the main idea of "History of Television"?

2 Which sentence from "Should We Watch TV?" best shows how the passages are different?

- **A** "The airwaves are flooded with all kinds of programs."
- **B** "There are hundreds of channels to choose from."
- **C** "And there's so much to see!"
- **D** "But if you are watching four hours a day, think about doing something else!"

How do the titles of the passages help you find the main idea of each? How are the key details in "History of Television" different from the most important ideas in "Should We Watch TV?"

3 State the main idea of each passage. Explain how those main ideas are different. Write a paragraph describing the main idea of each passage and tell how they are different.

_____

_____

_____

_____

_____

_____

_____

_____

_____

_____

Read the articles. Then answer the questions that follow.

E-Readers No Substitute for Real Books

by Linda Timm

1   It's a stormy, rainy, blustery day. You have a warm drink and a snack. Time to curl up with a good book and read. The window is nice and bright even though it's cloudy outside. You pull out your e-reader. Whoops—the battery is dead. And guess what? The storm has knocked the electricity out, so there's no recharging it, either. Guess you're out of luck.

2   This is just one example that shows how impractical e-readers are. E-readers are great toys, if you can afford one. They are pricey. Sure, they can hold thousands of books, but what good is that if the thing runs out of battery power right when you need it? And they are thin—sometimes lighter than a pound. That makes them super easy to break. Imagine how frustrating it would be to lose all of those books and have to pay for another e-reader!

3   Some schools are buying e-readers for students. This seems an unnecessary expense when most schools already have libraries full of thousands of real books. Most towns also have libraries that lend books. It seems that some people just aren't satisfied unless they have the latest gadget. This makes them feel more modern and "21st century." Well, the truth about technology is that sometimes the simplest solution is the best one.

4   A good school librarian is a treasure. She can help you locate sources for a class report, or just help you pick out a good book. If schools start replacing real books with e-readers, what will be the next step? Getting rid of librarians? Getting rid of the library altogether? Armed with those thousands of book titles to sift through, who will these students look to for help? There's only so much information that can be gathered from the Internet, after all. Sometimes, a human being is needed.

5   Books are inexpensive, recyclable, and portable. They are easy to distribute, easy to care for, and easy to replace. Many hundreds of thousands of books are free and available at your local library. And the best part? The batteries will NEVER run out of power!

from "Goodbye Books?"

by Jamie Joyce, Time for Kids

1   Cushing Academy used to have 20,000 books in its library. But over the summer, this small Massachusetts high school began to replace printed books with electronic books, or e-books. Why? "The school wanted to put its focus on 21st-century learning," Tom Corbett, the library's executive director, told TFK. Few students were using library books to do their school assignments. Most did their research online. Transforming the library seemed like the best way to meet students' needs. Without a print collection to care for, Corbett says librarians can now concentrate on helping students use the online collection in new and better ways. They can also work with teachers to bring technology into the classroom.

More Books, More Reading

2   Teacher Nancy Boyle says her students still enjoy regular books. But they're also testing out the Kindle, an electronic reader. So far, it's been a success. "It's great," Boyle told TFK. "The kids are reading more."

3   Sixteen-year-old Meghan Chenausky was skeptical at first. "I love the feeling of books," she told TFK. "I really thought I was going to be missing out when I started using a Kindle. But now I absolutely love using it. It's so convenient. You can have so many books right at your fingertips."

Meet an E-Reader

4   Can your backpack fit 1,500 books? An e-reader can. Most e-readers are pencil-thin and weigh less than a pound. They can download an e-book in 60 seconds. Don't understand the meaning of a word? Click on it to get the definition. Is the print too small? An e-reader can adjust the size.

5   E-readers aren't cheap, but it costs the school just $5 or $10 to download an e-book on as many as six e-readers. "Now, students have access to a million titles," Corbett says.

6   Still, regular books have one big advantage over e-readers: They don't use electricity. E-readers have to be charged, like cell phones.

1   How are the main ideas of these two passages **different**?

   A   "Goodbye Books?" is about Cushing Academy, while "E-Readers No Substitute for Real Books" is about libraries that have only real books.

   B   "Goodbye Books?" tells that e-readers are good for students and schools, while "E-Readers No Substitute for Real Books" tells that e-readers cannot replace real books.

   C   "Goodbye Books?" only discusses e-books, while "E-Readers No Substitute for Real Books" is only about real books.

   D   "Goodbye Books?" is about the low cost of e-readers, while "E-Readers No Substitute for Real Books" is about the low cost of real books.

2   What key detail can you find in **both** passages?

   A   An e-reader can hold 1,500 books.

   B   Most students do their research online.

   C   E-reader batteries have to be charged with electricity.

   D   Downloading a book onto an e-reader costs between $5 and $10.

3   Paragraph 4 in "Goodbye Books?" and paragraph 2 in "E-Readers No Substitute for Real Books" both tell that the e-book is thin and weighs less than a pound. Using two details from the texts, explain how the passages use this same detail to support **different** opinions.

_____

_____

_____

_____

4   Which sentence from "E-Readers No Substitute for Real Books" **best** shows
      how the two passages are **different**?

> **A**   "This is just one example that shows how impractical e-readers are."
>
> **B**   "Some schools are buying e-readers for students."
>
> **C**   "Most towns also have libraries that lend books."
>
> **D**   "There's only so much information that can be gathered from the Internet,
>   after all."

5   Read the sentences below. Then answer the question that follows.

> In the first article, Linda Timm says, "Some schools are buying e-readers for
> students. This seems an unnecessary expense when most schools already have
> libraries full of thousands of real books."

> In the second article, Jamie Joyce says, "E-readers aren't cheap, but it costs
> the school just $5 or $10 to download an e-book on as many as six e-readers."

Write a paragraph telling how these details show the difference between the
authors' point of view. Use **one** detail from each text to support your answer.

_____

_____

_____

_____

_____

_____

_____

 **Self Check**   *Go back and see what you can check off on the Self Check on page 169.*

Signs in the Sky

by Michelle August

1   Today, every news channel has a weather person. They can predict the weather for days, even weeks in advance. The science of meteorology involves using special machines to track weather systems. But long before people had this kind of technology, they could predict the weather. How did they do it? By observing the natural world.

2   For as long as people have grown their own food, they have wanted to predict the weather. Knowing the signs that told of coming rain or storms was important. Over many centuries, human beings learned to watch the sky for signs of coming weather. They even made up special sayings to help them remember the signs. Today, modern scientists have discovered something. Some of those old-fashioned sayings were right!

Red sky in the morning, sailors take warning. Red sky at night, sailors' delight.

3   This is a weather saying that is at least half right. Storm systems usually move from west to east. A red sunset in the west usually means that a high pressure system, or dry weather, is coming. Sunrises, on the other hand, can be red for a variety of reasons. Today, weather satellites track the movement of storms. But it is still fun to remember the old saying!

Ring around the moon, rain's coming soon.

4   Sometimes the moon appears to have a ring around it. This happens when there are high clouds in the sky. Those high clouds contain water and ice. The moonlight shines through the tiny pieces of ice. They make the halo appear. That same water and ice can soon fall as rain. So, this old saying is another one that "rings" true!

When clouds appear like rocks and towers, the earth's refreshed with frequent showers.

5   Have you ever watched clouds? Some clouds are thin and spread out. These are called cumulus clouds. They rarely carry rain. Other clouds are called cumulonimbus clouds. Strong winds cause these clouds to grow tall like towers. Heavy water in the clouds makes them look dark like rocks. These clouds almost always bring storms.

6   Today, we have all kinds of technology to predict the weather. Weather satellites travel into space. Weather software tracks storm patterns. But if all else fails, just look at the sky. The signs are there!

Mapping Sunshine and Rain

by Krista O'Connell

1   Weather is important to all people. A farmer's field can be ruined if the weather is hot and dry. A picnic can be spoiled by rain. People like to know what the weather will be like tomorrow, three days from now, and even next week. This is now possible thanks to the science of meteorology.

The Weather Map

2   One of the tools used to predict the weather is a weather map. Scientists use special machines to create these maps. These machines are used to collect information about conditions in the sky.

What Weather Maps Can Tell Us

3   A weather map might look complicated. But the truth is that most people can make weather predictions using a map like the sample one at the bottom of the next page. You just need to know what the shapes, symbols, and letters mean. Look at the map as you read along.

4   First, a weather map shows the places where weather fronts are found. Two main types of fronts are warm fronts and cold fronts. Both form when cooler air and hotter air meet. The map shows the symbols for each type of front. Warm fronts often bring rain and clouds. Cold fronts bring clear skies and cooler weather.

5   Second, a weather map shows any weather systems in the area. These can be high pressure or low pressure systems. They are shown on the map by the letters H and L. Both types move from west to east. High pressure systems often result in nice, sunny weather. Low pressure systems are likely to cause rain.

6   Third, maps show what type of weather these fronts and systems will cause. The map shows that the cold front in Denver is expected to bring snow. The cold front between Atlanta and Miami will likely bring showers and thunderstorms.

Replacing Signs in the Sky with Sound Science

7   It's true that looking into the sky can give some clues about what the weather will be in the near future. Most of us have seen the dark clouds that fill the sky before a thunderstorm. The color of the sky and the look of the moon can provide other clues.

8   People no longer have to make a guess about the weather. There are now maps like the one below as well as other tools. These can help meteorologists[1] make very exact weather forecasts. They can also help predict the weather well before it ever arrives.

[1] **meteorologists:** scientists who study and predict weather

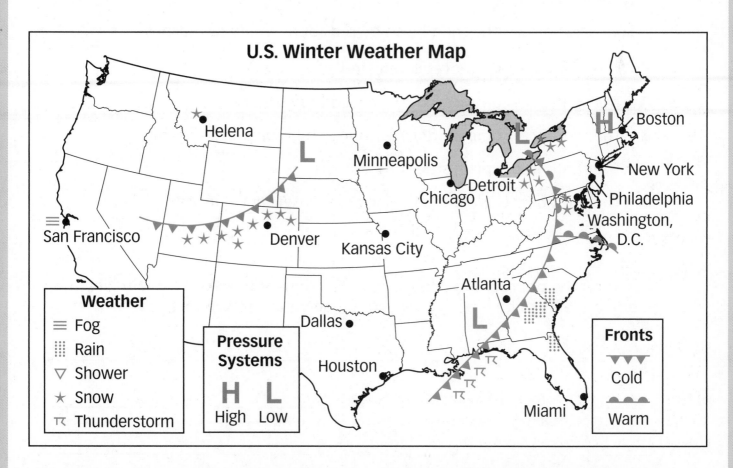

U.S. Winter Weather Map

1 Which of the following sentences from "Signs in the Sky" **best** describes the photograph on page 206?

  A "The moonlight shines through the tiny pieces of ice."

  B "Some of those old-fashioned sayings were right!"

  C "Strong winds cause these clouds to grow tall like towers."

  D "Weather software tracks storm patterns."

2 Read these two sentences from paragraph 3 of "Signs in the Sky."

  A red sunset in the west usually means that a high pressure system, or dry weather, is coming.

  Sunrises, on the other hand, can be red for a variety of reasons.

  How are these two sentences connected?

  A The sentences contrast red sunsets and red sunrises.

  B The sentences compare dry weather to high pressure systems.

  C The sentences explain steps in a process.

  D The sentences explain the reasons for sunsets and sunrises.

3 Based on the photograph and the text of "Signs in the Sky," explain why the moon appears to have a ring around it. Use details to support your answer.

_____

_____

_____

4   On the map, look at the low pressure system next to Denver. Now reread paragraph 6 of "Mapping Sunshine and Rain." What kind of weather is expected in Denver because of this low pressure system?

   A   fog

   B   snow

   C   rain

   D   thunderstorms

5   Read these three sentences from paragraph 4 of "Mapping Sunshine and Rain."

   Both form when cooler air and hotter air meet.

   Warm fronts often bring rain and clouds.

   Cold fronts bring clear skies and cooler weather.

   How are these sentences connected?

   A   The sentences describe how warm fronts cause cold fronts.

   B   The sentences describe three steps in a process.

   C   The sentences compare and contrast clouds and cooler weather.

   D   The sentences compare and contrast warm fronts and cold fronts.

6   Which key detail can you find in **both** passages?

   A   A ring around the moon shows that rain is coming.

   B   Weather systems move from west to east.

   C   Warm fronts often bring rain and clouds.

   D   A star symbol is used to stand for snow.

7 Answer Parts A, B, and C below.

Part A

How are the main ideas of "Signs in the Sky" and "Mapping Sunshine and Rain" **alike**?

A They are both about tools a meteorologist uses.

B They are both about tracking pressure systems.

C They are both about old-fashioned weather sayings.

D They are both about predicting weather.

Part B

Find a sentence in "Signs in the Sky" with details that support your response to Part A. Write that sentence on the lines below.

_____

_____

_____

Part C

Find a sentence in "Mapping Sunshine and Rain" with details that support your response to Part A. Write that sentence on the lines below.

_____

_____

_____

Performance Task—Extended Response

8 How are the main ideas "Signs in the Sky" and "Mapping Sunshine and Rain" different? Be sure to include key details from the text and the pictures of both passages to support your answer.

In your answer, be sure to
- identify the main idea of "Signs in the Sky."
- identify the main idea of "Mapping Sunshine and Rain."
- use key details from each passage to explain how the main ideas are different.

Check your writing for correct spelling, grammar, capitalization, and punctuation.

Use the space below to plan your essay.

Write your essay on the lines below.

_____

_____

_____

_____

_____

_____

_____

_____

_____

_____

_____

_____

Have you ever read more than one story or book that has the same character? Maybe you've read some of the *Magic Tree House* books, or maybe *Homer Price* or *Judy Moody*. In each story, the characters have a new problem or adventure. The same characters appear in each book. But where the stories take place, and what happens, changes. When you read these books, you share an adventure with the characters. You don't just read the words in the story, but you look at the pictures, too. From the pictures, you learn more about what the characters think and feel. You predict what the characters might do next. Reading books in a series makes reading an adventure.

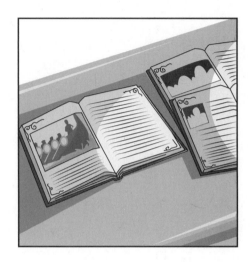

In this unit, you will practice looking at the details in pictures. In the pictures, you'll find clues about the characters, the setting, and the message of each story. You'll read several stories about one character. And you'll notice what is alike and different about the stories. One thing's for sure—it will be an adventure!

✓ Self Check

Before starting this unit, check off the skills you know below. As you complete each lesson, see how many more you can check off!

I know how to:	Before this unit	After this unit
explain how pictures in a story help me understand the story's characters.	☐	☐
explain how pictures in a story help me understand the story's setting.	☐	☐
explain how pictures in a story help me understand the mood of a story.	☐	☐
compare and contrast the settings of stories written by the same author about the same characters.	☐	☐
compare and contrast the plots and themes of stories written by the same author about the same characters.	☐	☐

Lesson 21   Part 1: Introduction

Connecting Words and Pictures

CCSS

RL.3.7: Explain how specific aspects of a text's illustrations contribute to what is conveyed by the words in a story (e.g., create mood, emphasize aspects of a character or setting).

Theme: *Stories That Amaze*

The **pictures** that go with a story can show you how the **characters** feel and what the **setting** looks like. The words and pictures in a story also create the **mood**, or the feeling a story gives you. Stories can have all kinds of moods: happy, sad, excited, bored, calm, spooky, silly, and so on.

The picture below shows a girl and a boy walking through the woods. They can hear wolves howling, owls hooting, and bats screeching.

What feeling do you get from the picture and the words that describe it?

_____

Look at the chart below to see how pictures and words work together in a story.

	Characters	**Setting**	**Mood**
Picture	The children look worried.	The woods look dark and dangerous.	spooky
Words	They are hearing animal sounds.	Wolves, owls, and bats are making sounds.	

How would the mood of this story be different if the picture showed the children laughing and the woods full of sunlight? The mood would be happy instead of spooky.

Pictures in stories give information about mood, setting, and what characters think and feel. Good readers pay attention to both pictures and words as they read.

Read the first part of a tall tale about Pecos Bill and look at the picture.

When Pecos Bill Was Young *by Walt Bisco*

Right from the day he was born, Pecos Bill was not much like other kids. He had eighteen older brothers and sisters. When he was just a baby, he jumped on a horse and rode it alongside his family's covered wagon as they traveled West. Oh, and Bill also wrestled bears! Bill's family was sure he would lead an amazing life.

(continued)

Explore how to answer this question: *"What do the details in the picture help you better understand about Pecos Bill?"*

The question asks how the picture helps you "better understand" Pecos Bill. This means that you need to look for details in the picture that the story does not tell you.

- The story tells that the baby Pecos Bill rode a horse alongside his family's covered wagon.
- The picture shows a running horse being ridden by a baby.
- The baby is laughing and waving his arm while riding the horse.
- The details in the picture show that Pecos Bill was very unusual when he was a baby.

Fill in the blanks below to tell how details in the picture help you better understand Pecos Bill.

In the picture, baby Pecos Bill is laughing and waving his _____ while riding

a running _____ . These details in the picture help show that Pecos Bill

was a very _____ baby.

Continue reading about Pecos Bill. Use the Close Reading and the Hint to help you answer the question.

Close Reading

Underline the sentence that tells what is happening in the picture.

(continued from page 216)

One time, the wagon went over a big bump, and Bill was launched into the air and far, far away. After he landed on the soft ground, a mother coyote spotted Bill. She took Bill back to her den and raised him as one of her own. For a long time, Bill didn't know he *wasn't* a coyote.

Hint

What is the feeling on Bill's face? What are the coyote pups doing?

Circle the correct answer.

Based on details in the picture, what is the mood of this part of the story?

A nervous, because the coyotes want to harm Pecos Bill

B sad, because Pecos Bill misses his human family

C cheerful, because Pecos Bill looks happy to be with the coyotes

D silly, because Pecos Bill is trying to trick the coyotes

✎ Show Your Thinking

Look at the answer you chose above. What details from the picture helped you name the mood of the story?

_____

_____

💬 Think about the last sentence of the story: "For a long time, Bill didn't know he *wasn't* a coyote." Tell your partner how the picture helps you understand this sentence.

Read the tall tale and look at the picture. Use the Study Buddy and Close Reading to guide your reading.

The picture shows an event from the story. I'm going to use the picture to help me better understand what happens in the story.

Close Reading

How is the event shown in the picture described in the story? **Underline** the sentence that tells about this event.

Is Paul Bunyan helpful? **Circle** a sentence that tells what he decides to do for the pioneers.

Genre: **Tall Tale**

from "Paul Bunyan"
by Mary Pope Osborne, American Tall Tales

1　　Paul Bunyan and Babe the Blue Ox were inseparable. Babe grew so fast that Paul liked to close his eyes for a minute, count to ten, then look to see how much Babe had grown. Sometimes the ox would be a whole foot taller.

2　　In those times, huge sections of America were filled with dark green forests. And the forests were filled with trees— oceans of trees—trees as far as the eye could see.

3　　It would be nice if those trees could have stayed tall and thick forever. But the pioneers needed them to build houses, churches, ships, wagons, bridges, and barns. So one day Paul Bunyan took a good look at all those trees and said "Babe, stand back. I'm about to invent logging."

4　　*"Tim-ber!"* he yelled, and he swung his bright steel ax in a wide circle. There was a terrible crash, and when Paul looked around, he saw he'd felled ten white pines with a single swing.

Hints

What details in the picture add to the story's description of Paul Bunyan?

Use the Hints on this page to help you answer the questions.

1 What does the picture tell you about Paul Bunyan?

A Paul Bunyan built houses for the pioneers.

B Paul Bunyan was about twice as tall as the trees.

C Paul Bunyan lived in the time of the pioneers.

D Paul Bunyan and his ox were not always together.

What is Paul about to do in the picture?

2 Which sentence from the story tells a detail that is shown in the picture?

A "Sometimes the ox would be a whole foot taller."

B "It would be nice if those trees could have stayed tall and thick forever."

C "But the pioneers needed them to build houses, churches, ships, wagons, bridges, and barns."

D "'Tim-ber!' he yelled, and he swung his bright steel ax in a wide circle."

Why does Paul invent logging? What does this tell you about his character?

3 Use the story and the picture to describe **two** details that help explain what Paul Bunyan is like.

Detail from the story that helps me understand what Paul is like:

_____

_____

_____

_____

Detail from the picture that helps me understand what Paul is like:

_____

_____

_____

_____

Read the tall tale. Then answer the questions that follow.

from "Stormalong"

by Mary Pope Osborne, American Tall Tales

1　　One day in the early 1800s a tidal wave crashed down on the shores of Cape Cod in New England. After the wave had washed back out to sea, the villagers heard deep, bellowing sounds coming from the beach. When they rushed to find out what was going on, they couldn't believe their eyes. A giant baby three fathoms tall—or eighteen feet!—was crawling across the sand, crying in a voice as loud as a foghorn.

2　　The villagers put the baby in a big wheelbarrow and carried him to town. They took him to the meetinghouse and fed him barrels and barrels of milk. As ten people patted the baby on the back, the minister said, "What will we name him?"

3　　"How about *Alfred Bulltop Stormalong*!" a little boy piped up.

4　　"And call him Stormy for short."

5　　The baby smiled at the boy, then let out a giant burp that nearly blew the roof off the meetinghouse.

6　　"Stormy it is!" everyone cried.

7　　By the time Stormy was twelve, he was already six fathoms tall—or thirty-six feet! "I guess you're going to have to go out into the world now," his friends said sadly. "Maybe you should go to Boston. It's a lot bigger than Cape Cod."

8　　"A sailor's life is the only one for me," he said, staring longingly at Boston Harbor. "The sea's my best friend. It's with her that I belong." And with his back to Boston, Stormy strode toward the biggest Yankee clipper docked in the harbor, *The Lady of the Sea*.

9   "Blow me down!" said the captain when Stormy stood before him. "I've never seen a man as big as you before."

10   "I'm not a man," said Stormy. "I'm twelve years old."

11   "Blow me down again!" said the captain. "I guess you'll have to be the biggest cabin boy in the world then. Welcome aboard, son."

12   The sailors were a bit shocked when the captain introduced the thirty-six-foot giant as their new cabin boy. But the day soon came when all the sailors of *The Lady of the Sea* completely accepted Stormy's awesome size. It happened one morning when the clipper was anchored off the coast of South America.

13   "Hoist the anchor!" the captain shouted after a few hours of deep-sea fishing. But when the crew pulled on the great chain, nothing happened. The sailors heaved and hoed, and still could not move the anchor off the bottom of the ocean.

14   "Let me take care of it!" Stormy boomed. Then the cabin boy stuck a knife between his teeth, climbed onto the bowsprit, and dived into the sea.

15   After Stormy disappeared, terrible sounds came from the water. The ship began pitching and tossing on wild, foaming waves. It seemed that all aboard were about to be hurled to a wet grave, when suddenly the sea grew calm again—and Stormy bobbed to the surface.

16   "What happened?" cried the crew.

17   "Just a little fight with a two-ton octopus," said Stormy.

18   "Octopus!"

19   "Aye. He didn't want to let go of our anchor."

20   "What'd you do to him?" the others cried.

21   "Wrestled eight slimy tentacles into double knots. It'll take a month o' Sundays for him to untie himself."

22   From then on Stormy was the most popular sailor on board.

Answer Form

1 Ⓐ Ⓑ Ⓒ Ⓓ **Number**
2 Ⓐ Ⓑ Ⓒ Ⓓ **Correct** /2

1 Based on the picture and the description of Stormy burping, which of these **best** tells the mood of this part of the story?

   A serious

   B funny

   C scary

   D quiet

2 Which sentence from the story is most closely related to the picture of Stormy about to dive into the sea?

   A "The villagers put the baby in a big wheelbarrow and carried him to town."

   B "How about *Alfred Bulltop Stormalong*!" a little boy piped up.

   C "'Let me take care of it!' Stormy boomed."

   D "After Stormy disappeared, terrible sounds came from the water."

3 Use the story and the pictures to describe Stormy. Use **one** detail from the story and **one** detail from either picture to support your answer.

_____

_____

_____

_____

_____

_____

✓ **Self Check** *Go back and see what you can check off on the Self Check on page 213.*

Comparing and Contrasting Stories

CCSS
RL.3.9: Compare and contrast the themes, settings, and plots of stories written by the same author about the same or similar characters (e.g., in books from a series).

Theme: *Stories That Teach*

Some authors use the same characters or similar characters in many of their stories. These stories might be in a **series**, or a set of books connected by their characters.

Although the characters may be the same, each story in a series may have a different **setting** where the action takes place. The **plots**, or the way the events in stories happen, may also be different. You can also compare the **themes**, or the central message about life the stories offer.

Look at the titles and pictures from a book series called *The Adventures of Super Cat!* Think about what is similar between the pictures and what is different.

Book 1: Super Cat Rescues a Kitten	Book 2: Super Cat Stops a Volcano from Erupting

Look at the chart below. It compares and contrasts the two books about Super Cat.

	Book 1	**Book 2**
Setting	Empire State Building, New York City	a volcano
Plot	Super Cat rescues a kitten.	Super Cat stops a volcano from erupting.
Theme	Use your powers to do good things.	Use your powers to do good things.

Good readers notice what is the same and what is different about the settings, plots, and themes of stories that have the same or similar characters.

Read the descriptions of the next two books about Super Cat.

Genre: **Fantasy**

Book 3: Super Cat Climbs Mount Everest

Super Cat travels to the highest mountain to save frightened climbers from a snow monster. He meets the monster and learns it is a baby creature who has lost its mother. Super Cat helps it find its family. The climbers feel safe again.

Book 4: Super Cat Discovers a Planet

Super Cat lands on an uncharted planet full of angry people. They are so grumpy that Super Cat decides to leave the planet. But then he learns that all their water has disappeared. No wonder they're unhappy! Using his superhero glasses, he finds a new underground water source. The people are saved—and much friendlier.

(continued)

Explore how to answer this question: *"What theme do both books have in common?"*

These books have different settings and plots, but they share a similar message. Identifying the main problem in the plot and how it is solved will help you find the theme of a story.

Fill in the blanks to complete the chart about the problem and solution in each story.

Book	What is the problem?	How is the problem solved?	Why is the problem solved?
3	A snow _____ is scaring a group of mountain climbers.	Super Cat helps the baby creature find its _____ .	Super Cat learns the snow monster is a lost _____ _____ .
4	All the _____ on a planet has disappeared.	Super Cat uses superhero _____ to find water for the people.	Super Cat decides to stay on the planet and help after learning why the people are angry.

Fill in the blank below to write about the theme of both books.

The theme in both books is that understanding others can help solve _____ .

Read the description of the fifth Super Cat book. Use the Close Reading and the Hint to help you answer the question.

Close Reading

What does Super Cat do when he learns that an important statue is missing? **Underline** the sentence that tells what happens when he finds the statue.

(continued from page 224)

Book 5: Super Cat Goes to Egypt

Super Cat visits the pyramids in Egypt. He learns that a treasured cat statue is missing. To get a better view of the desert, Super Cat climbs the tallest pyramid. Wearing his superhero glasses, he can see something miles away, partly buried in sand. It's the cat statue! His earth-shaking "Meow!" alerts authorities and the statue is rescued.

Hint

What does Super Cat do in all of the books?

Circle the correct answer.

Based on Books 1 through 4 of the Super Cat series, what would be another good title for Book 5?

A Super Cat Has a Mighty Meow

B Super Cat Uses His Superhero Glasses

C Once Again, Super Cat Saves the Day

D Once Again, Super Cat Climbs a Pyramid

 Show Your Thinking

Look at the answer you just chose. Pick one detail from each of the five Super Cat book descriptions that supports your answer.

_____

_____

_____

_____

Imagine that you have been asked to write the next Super Cat book in the series. Tell your partner your idea for this book.

Read the passages from a famous epic story. Use the Study Buddies and the Close Reading to guide your reading.

Ulysses and his crew are in both stories, but the plots are different. I'm going to look for other ways the stories are alike and different.

Close Reading

Why does the crew want to open the bag? **Circle** words that tell what the crew thinks is in the bag.

How do Ulysses's men change the outcome of the story? **Underline** a sentence that shows what they do.

Genre: **Epic**

from "The Home of the Winds"
retold from Homer's The Odyssey *by Alfred J. Church*

1   The next day Ulysses and his companions set sail. After a while they came to the floating island where the King of the Winds had his home. For a whole month the king made him welcome.

2   When Ulysses wished to go home, the king did what he could to help him. He took the hide of an ox, very thick and strong. He put in it all the winds that would keep Ulysses from getting to his home, and he fastened it to the deck of his ship. Then he made a gentle wind blow from the west. For nine days it blew, till the ships were very near to the island of Ithaca.

3   But just before dawn on the tenth day, Ulysses, who had stayed awake all the time, fell asleep. The crew of his ship said to each other: "See that great bag of ox hide. It must have something very precious inside it—silver and gold and jewels. Why should the chief have all these good things to himself?"

4   So they cut the bag open, and all the winds rushed out and blew the ship away from Ithaca. Ulysses woke up at the noise, and at first thought that he would throw himself into the sea and die. Then he said to himself, "No! It is better to live," and he covered his face and lay still, without saying a word to his men. And the ships were driven back to the island of the King of the Winds.

from "Ulysses and the Sirens"

retold from Homer's The Odyssey *by Alfred J. Church*

1   The first place they came to was the Island of Sirens. The Sirens were mermaids who sang so sweetly that no one who heard them could pass on his way, but was forced to go to them. But when he came near, the Sirens flew upon him and tore him to pieces.

2   Now Circe had warned Ulysses about these dreadful creatures, and told him what he ought to do. So he closed the ears of his companions with wax so tightly that they could hear nothing. As for himself, he made his men tie him with ropes to the mast of the ship. "And see," he said, "that you don't loose me, however much I may beg and pray."

3   As soon as the ship came near to the island, the wind ceased to blow. The men took down the sails and began to row.

4   Then the Sirens saw the ship and began to sing. Ulysses, where he stood bound to the mast, heard them. And when he understood what they said, he forgot all his caution. They promised just the thing that he wanted. For he was a man who thought he could never know enough about other countries and the people who dwelt in them. And the Sirens said that they could tell him all this.

5   Then he made signs with his head to his men that they should loose him. But they remembered what he had told them and rowed on. So they got safely past the Island of the Sirens.

Ulysses sure goes to a lot of trouble to hear the Sirens sing. I think Ulysses likes to learn new things, even when they're dangerous.

Close Reading

Ulysses protects his crew from the Sirens. **Underline** a sentence that shows how his crew helps him in return.

How does the crew protect Ulysses when he wants to be untied from the mast? **Draw a box** around the paragraph that tells how the crew keeps Ulysses safe from the Sirens.

Hints

In both stories, how do Ulysses and his men travel from place to place?

What makes Ulysses upset in "The Home of the Winds"?

Think about how the crew's actions led to success or failure in the two stories.

Use the Hints on this page to help you answer the questions.

1 How are the settings of the two stories alike?

   A   Both stories take place on or near islands.

   B   Both stories take place in the home of a king.

   C   Both stories take place on land far from the sea.

   D   Both stories take place in Ulysses's home.

2 Which of these best explains how the actions of Ulysses's crew in "The Home of the Winds" is different from their actions in "Ulysses and the Sirens"?

   A   In "The Home of the Winds," the crew obeys Ulysses.

   B   In "The Home of the Winds," the crew betrays Ulysses.

   C   In "The Home of the Winds," the crew makes Ulysses happy.

   D   In "The Home of the Winds," the crew ties Ulysses to the mast.

3 A theme of both stories is that leaders can succeed only when they can depend on their followers. Write two details from each story that show how this theme is true for both stories.

_____

_____

_____

_____

_____

_____

_____

_____

_____

_____

Read the two passages from a famous epic story. Then answer the questions that follow.

from "The Cyclops"

retold from Homer's The Odyssey *by Alfred J. Church*

1   One of Ulysses's many adventures was in the country of the Cyclops or Round-eyed People. While exploring the country, he and his men came to a cave. Inside there were pens for sheep and baskets full of cheeses. Ulysses's men said to him: "Let us go away before the master comes back." But Ulysses would not listen to them. He wanted to see what kind of man this shepherd might be.

2   In the evening the Cyclops came home. He was a great giant, with one big eye in the middle of his forehead. He drove his flocks inside and then closed up the mouth of the cave with a rock so big that twenty wagons could not carry it.

3   When the giant saw the men, he grabbed up two of them and swallowed them. Then he lay down among his sheep and slept.

4   Ulysses thought: "Shall I slay this monster as he sleeps? But no; if I do this, we will be trapped. Who shall be able to roll away the great rock that is against the mouth of the cave?"

5   The giant left early the next morning, but kept the sheep and the men in the cave by rolling the rock back in place. All day, Ulysses and his men worked on a plan to escape the cave. In the evening, the giant came back. He grabbed two more men and swallowed them. When he had finished, Ulysses came to him with a special drink in his hand and said, "Drink, Cyclops, now that you have eaten."

6   The Cyclops took the glass and drank. "Give me more," he said, "and tell me your name."

7   Then Ulysses said: "My name is No Man."

8   When the giant fell asleep, Ulysses threw the spear he and his men had made into the giant's one eye. The giant leapt up and cried out so loudly that the Round-eyed people on the island came to see what had happened.

9   "Is someone hurting you?" they asked.

10   The giant bellowed, "No Man is hurting me!"

11   "Well," said the Round-eyed people, "if no man is hurting you, then it must be the gods that do it. We cannot help you against them."

12   Now Ulysses had made a plan to escape the cave. He took the biggest sheep and tied the men underneath their bellies. For himself, he clung to the belly of a sheep with both hands. When morning came, the flocks went out of the cave. The giant, now blind, felt them as they passed, but he did not feel the men.

from "The Dangerous Way"

retold from Homer's The Odyssey *by Alfred J. Church*

1   There was a narrow place between the mainland and an island. On the one side there was a cave, in which there lived a terrible monster named Scylla. On the other side, there was a dreadful whirlpool called Charybdis. If a ship ever got into that, it was sucked down to the bottom of the sea and never came up again.

2   Circe had told Ulysses what he should do. "It will be better," she had said, "to go near Scylla than to go near Charybdis. Scylla will pounce down upon your ship when it comes within her reach. She will take six men, one for each of the six heads that she has. But if you go too near to Charybdis, your whole ship will be swallowed up. It is better to lose six men than have all of them drown."

3   When Ulysses had said, "May I not take shield and spear and fight with this monster?" Circe had answered, "You are wonderfully bold. You would fight with the gods themselves. But be sure that you cannot fight with Scylla. She is too strong for any man. And while you linger she will take six more men. No. Fly from the place as fast as you can."

4   So now he told the steersman to steer the ship as near as he could to the side of the strait near Scylla's cave. Nevertheless, they went very close to the whirlpool. It was a wonderful sight. At one time, you could see to the very bottom of the sea. And at another time, the water seemed to boil up almost to the top of the cliffs.

5   Now, Ulysses had said nothing to his men about the monster on the other side. He was afraid that if they knew about her they would not go on with their voyage. So they all stood and watched the whirlpool. Then, suddenly, there came down upon the ship Scylla's dreadful hands. She caught up six of the crew, the bravest and strongest of them all. Ulysses heard them cry to him to help them, but he could do nothing. And this, he said afterwards, was the very saddest thing that happened to him in all his troubles.

Answer Form

1 Ⓐ Ⓑ Ⓒ Ⓓ
2 Ⓐ Ⓑ Ⓒ Ⓓ
3 Ⓐ Ⓑ Ⓒ Ⓓ   **Number** ___/4
4 Ⓐ Ⓑ Ⓒ Ⓓ   **Correct**

1   How are the settings of the stories **different**?

   A   "The Cyclops" takes place in a cave, and "The Dangerous Way" takes place on a ship.

   B   "The Cyclops" takes place in a field of sheep, and "The Dangerous Way" takes place on a ship.

   C   "The Cyclops" takes place on the sea, and "The Dangerous Way" takes place on land.

   D   "The Cyclops" takes place in a town, and "The Dangerous Way" takes place in a whirlpool.

2   In "The Cyclops," Ulysses blinds the giant with a spear. How is the way Ulysses deals with the monster in "The Dangerous Way" **different**?

   A   In "The Dangerous Way," he tricks the monster into staying in its cave.

   B   In "The Dangerous Way," he tells the monster its real name.

   C   In "The Dangerous Way," he doesn't fight the monster.

   D   In "The Dangerous Way," he avoids the monster by sailing into a whirlpool.

3   Which words **best** describe Ulysses in both stories?

   A   confused and frustrated

   B   brave and daring

   C   carefree and relaxed

   D   gloomy and upset

4   In "The Dangerous Way," Ulysses does not tell his men what will happen when they sail between Scylla and Charybdis. How is the way Ulysses treats his men in "The Cyclops" **different** from the way he treats them in "The Dangerous Way"?

   A   In "The Cyclops," he lets the giant eat his men so that he can escape.

   B   In "The Cyclops," he tricks his men into believing they are sheep.

   C   In "The Cyclops," he tells his men that the giant will eat him last.

   D   In "The Cyclops," he works together with his men to defeat the giant.

5   A theme of both stories is that great adventures involve great dangers. Write a paragraph telling how both stories have this theme. Use **one** detail from **each** story to support your answer.

   _____

   _____

   _____

   _____

   _____

   _____

 **Self Check**   *Go back and see what you can check off on the Self Check on page 213.*

Read the folktales. Then answer the questions that follow.

Anansi Tries to Steal
All the Wisdom in the World

a folktale from West Africa

1   Anansi the spider knew that he was not wise. He was a sly trickster who could use his wit to fool many different people. But he knew that he did not have much wisdom.

2   Then one day he had a clever thought. "If I can get all of the wisdom in the village and put it in a hollow gourd," he thought, "I will be very wise indeed. In fact, I will be the wisest of all!"

3   So he found a hollow gourd and began to carry out his plan. He went from door to door to collect the village's wisdom. People chuckled at poor Anansi, for they knew that more than any other creature, he needed wisdom. So each person put a bit of wisdom in his gourd and wished him well.

4   Soon the gourd was overflowing with wisdom and could hold no more. Now Anansi needed to find a place to store it. "I am certainly the wisest person in the world. But if I don't find a good hiding place for my wisdom, I am sure to lose it."

5   He looked around and spotted a very tall tree. "Ah," Anansi said, "I will hide my wisdom high in that tree. Then I will never have to worry about someone stealing it from me!"

6   Anansi set out to climb the towering tree with the heavy gourd tied to the front of his belly where it would be safe. As he climbed, however, the gourd full of wisdom kept getting in the way. He tried and tried, but he could not climb very high.

7   Just then, Anansi's youngest son walked by. "What are you doing, Father?" asked the little spider.

8   "I am climbing this tree with my gourd full of wisdom," Anansi replied.

9   "But Father," said the son, "wouldn't it be much easier if you tied the gourd behind you instead of in front?"

10   Anansi sat there quietly for a very long time. Then he said, "Shouldn't you be going home now?"

11   After his son left, Anansi moved the gourd so that it was behind him. Then he proceeded up the tree without a problem. When he reached the top, he cried out, "I collected so much wisdom that I am the wisest person ever, and still my baby son is wiser than me. Here! Take back your wisdom!"

12   He lifted the gourd high over his head and spilled its contents into the wind. The wisdom blew far and wide and settled across the land. And this is how wisdom came back to the world.

Anansi and the Lion

a folktale from West Africa

1   Anansi the spider caught some fish and cooked them. He put them in a sack to take into the forest, where he could eat them all himself. "These will taste delicious," he chuckled.

2   Anansi hadn't gone very far when he met Lion, and Lion asked him, "Well, brother Anansi, what have you got there?"

3   "Oh . . . just some old bones that I'm going to bury in the mountains."

4   Lion walked away, but then he started thinking. "I know that Anansi is a great trickster. He probably has something in that sack he doesn't want me to see. I will follow him to see what he's up to."

5   When Anansi got into the woods, he set his sack down, took out one fish, and ate it. He didn't think anyone else was around, so he took out another fish. But just then, Lion came up and said, "Well, brother Anansi, those don't look like bones to me. That was a pretty tale you told me."

6   "Oh! brother Lion, I am so glad you have come. Never mind what I told you—it was only my fun. Come and join me."

7 So Lion sat down and began to eat, and before Anansi had eaten one fish, Lion had almost emptied the sack. Anansi said to himself, "Greedy fellow, eating up all my fish!"

8 "What did you say, sir?"

9 "I said you do not eat fast enough," Anansi replied, for he was afraid of what Lion might do. Soon, all the fish were gone.

10 While Anansi didn't complain, he did want to get back at Lion for eating most of his fish. He had a clever thought. "Which of us do you think is the stronger?"

11 Lion said, "Why, I am, of course."

12 Then Anansi said, "We will tie one another to that tree, and we shall see who is the stronger."

13 Now they agreed that Lion should tie Anansi first, and he tied him with some very fine string, and not very tight. Anansi twisted himself two or three times, and the string broke.

14 Then it was Anansi's turn to tie Lion, and he took some very strong rope. Lion said, "You must not tie me tight, for I did not tie you tight."

15 And Anansi said, "Oh, no, to be sure, I will not!" But he tied him as tight as ever he could and then told him to try and get loose.

16 Lion tried and tried, but he could not get loose.

17 Anansi thought, "That is what he gets for eating my meal, and now it's time for me to leave. So Anansi took up his empty sack and left Lion behind, tied to the tree.

Answer the questions. Mark your answers to questions 1–6 on the Answer Form to the right.

1 Look at the picture in "Anansi Tries to Steal All the Wisdom in the World." What does the picture tell you about the way Anansi feels in this part of the story?

A He is proud because he got what he wanted.

B He is excited to see his young son.

C He is sad and unhappy because someone might steal from him.

D He is frustrated and bothered because he can't go faster.

2 Which word from "Anansi Tries to Steal All the Wisdom in the World" does the picture help you understand?

A village

B hollow

C gourd

D contents

3 Which of the following statements is true about Anansi in **both** stories?

A Anansi thinks he is foolish.

B Others think Anansi is foolish.

C Anansi thinks he is clever.

D Others think Anansi is clever.

4   Which statement is true about the setting in **both** stories?

    A   A tree is an important part of the setting.

    B   A village is an important part of the setting.

    C   The mountains are an important part of the setting.

    D   The sky is an important part of the setting.

5   Answer Parts A and B below.

Part A

What happens in the first picture from "Anansi and the Lion"?

    A   Anansi offers to share his fish with Lion.

    B   Anansi tells Lion he is carrying a bag of bones.

    C   Anansi has a contest of strength with Lion.

    D   Anansi gets upset when Lion eats most of the fish.

Part B

Which sentence from the story **best** supports the answer to Part A?

    A   "Oh! brother Lion, I am so glad you have come."

    B   "While Anansi didn't complain, he did want to get back at Lion for eating most of his fish."

    C   "When Anansi got into the woods, he set his sack down, took out one fish, and ate it."

    D   "Lion tried and tried, but he could not get loose."

6 Based on the text and the **second** picture in "Anansi and the Lion," which word describes the mood at the end of the story?

   A pleased

   B frightened

   C amazed

   D bored

7 A trickster is a type of character that likes to play tricks on others. Why is Anansi called a trickster in both stories? Use details from **both** stories to support your answer.

Write your answer in complete sentences.

_____

_____

_____

_____

_____

_____

_____

_____

Performance Task—Extended Response

8   In both stories, which characters are greedy? What do they want? Do they
     finally get what they want? Use details from each story to support your
     answer.

     In your answer, be sure to
     • tell which characters are greedy in each story
     • tell what the greedy characters want in each story
     • tell whether or not the greedy characters finally get what they want
     • use details from both stories in your answer

Check your writing for correct spelling, grammar, capitalization, and punctuation.

Use the space below to plan your essay.

Write your essay on the lines below.

_____

_____

_____

_____

_____

_____

_____

_____

_____

_____

_____

_____

_____

Ready® Common Core Language Handbook Table of Contents

Knowledge of Language

Vocabulary Acquisition and Use

CCSS
L.3.3a
L.3.3b
L.3.4a
L.3.4b
L.3.4c
L.3.4d
L.3.5a
L.3.5b
L.3.5c
L.3.6

Lesson 1
Nouns

CCSS
L.3.1a: Explain the function of nouns . . . in general and their functions in particular sentences.

Introduction A **noun** is a word that names a person, place, or thing.

- A **common noun** names any person, place, or thing.
- A **proper noun** names a particular person, place, or thing. A proper noun begins with a capital letter.

	Common Nouns	**Proper Nouns**
Person	girl, teacher, president	Emily, Mr. Wong, Abraham Lincoln
Place	street, lake, country	Pine Street, Lake Mead, Mexico
Thing	cereal, month, holiday	Crispies, April, Thanksgiving

Guided Practice Underline the nouns in each sentence. Write *person*, *place*, or *thing* above each noun to tell what it names.

Hint

A proper noun can be more than one word. Each important word in a proper noun begins with a capital letter.

1 Aunt Lisa takes us to Oak Park.

2 The big slide is near Vine Street.

3 Nicole climbs the ladder quickly.

4 Alex loves the green and blue swing.

5 My little brother plays in the sand.

6 My sister pulls her wagon beside the pond.

7 Our Koby Kite flies high in the sky.

8 My aunt always brings a Fruitybar to share.

For numbers 1–4, choose the correct word or words to answer each question.

1 Which words in this sentence are nouns?

Chase Pond is in the large park.

A Chase Pond, is

B the, park

C Chase Pond, park

D in, large

2 Which words in this sentence are nouns?

Mark and his sister often swim there.

A Mark, sister

B and, sister

C his, often

D Mark, swim

3 Which noun in this sentence names a person?

One day Meera saw a frog and a turtle.

A day

B Meera

C frog

D turtle

4 Which noun in this sentence names a place?

Ms. Patel and her friend enjoy having a picnic on the beach.

A Ms. Patel

B friend

C picnic

D beach

Lesson 2
Pronouns

CCSS
L.3.1a: Explain the function of . . . pronouns . . . in general and their functions in particular sentences.

Introduction   A **pronoun** is a word that can take the place of a noun. Use pronouns in your writing so you don't repeat the same noun over and over.

> Sonya rides horses. ~~Sonya~~ is a very good rider.
> ^{She} above "Sonya"

*Correction: Sonya rides horses. **She** is a very good rider.*

- **Subject pronouns** take the place of the subject of a sentence. The **subject** is the part of the sentence that tells whom or what the sentence is about.

> ~~Mr. Alvarez~~ gives riding lessons. ~~The lessons~~ are fun to learn.
> **He** above "Mr. Alvarez"; **They** above "The lessons"

- **Object pronouns** take the place of nouns that follow action verbs and words such as *to*, *in*, *at*, *on*, and *for*.

> Horses love ~~Mr. Alvarez~~. Mr. Alvarez is kind to ~~horses~~.
> **him** above "Mr. Alvarez"; **them** above "horses"

	Subject Pronouns	Object Pronouns
Singular	I, you, he, she, it	me, you, him, her, it
Plural	we, you, they	us, you, them

Guided Practice   Circle the correct pronoun to take the place of the underlined word or words.

Hint

Use a singular pronoun to replace a noun that tells about one person, place, or thing. Use a plural pronoun to replace a noun that tells about two or more people, places, or things.

1. <u>Sonya</u> has been riding for six years.

    Her   It   **She**

2. Mr. Alvarez found a gentle horse for <u>Sonya's brother</u>.

    he   **him**   they

3. Asa got in the saddle. He sat up straight in <u>the saddle</u>.

    him   you   **it**

4. Now <u>Sonya and Asa</u> go riding together.

    them   **they**   she

For numbers 1–5, choose the correct pronoun to take the place of the underlined words in the sentence.

1 The horses are beautiful.

A It

B They

C Them

D We

2 The stable is my sister's favorite place.

A Them

B You

C He

D It

3 The riding teachers love my sister.

A it

B they

C us

D her

4 Mr. Chen gives fresh hay to the horses.

A they

B him

C them

D it

5 Mr. Chen owns the stable.

A He

B They

C Him

D Them

Lesson 3
Verbs

CCSS
L.3.1a: Explain the function of . . . verbs . . . in general and their functions in particular sentences.

Introduction A **verb** is a word that tells what someone or something *does* or *is*.

- Some verbs show action. An **action verb** tells what someone or something does.

  Squirrels eat nuts and leaves. I watch the squirrels in the tree.

- Some verbs do <u>not</u> show action. The verb *be* tells what someone or something is. The verb *be* has different forms. *Am, is,* and *are* are all forms of *be*.

Forms of *Be*	Examples
am	I am an expert on squirrels.
is	A tree is a good home for squirrels. Is it a safe place to hide? Yes, it is.
are	Most squirrels are brown or gray. They are so cute!

Guided Practice Underline the verb in each sentence. Write *A* above the verb if it is an action verb. Write *B* if it is a form of the verb *be*.

Hint
In a question, the verb *be* can come at the beginning of the sentence.

Example: Is it furry?

1. Squirrels live in cities and in the country.

2. Are you afraid of squirrels?

3. I am not afraid of them.

4. I study different kinds of squirrels.

5. Indian giant squirrels grow as long as three feet!

6. A pygmy squirrel is five inches long.

7. Most gray squirrels eat acorns in fall and winter.

8. Is that a gray squirrel in the tree?

For numbers 1–5, choose the word in each sentence that is a verb.

1 Some squirrels glide through the air.

A Some

B through

C glide

D air

2 They stretch their arms and legs.

A They

B arms

C and

D stretch

3 Their tails are flat and wide.

A tails

B Their

C wide

D are

4 Is that a squirrel or a bat?

A squirrel

B Is

C that

D bat

5 Mary wrote her report about those squirrels.

A Mary

B wrote

C her

D about

Lesson 4
Adjectives

CCSS
L.3.1a: Explain the function of . . . adjectives . . . in general and their functions in particular sentences.

Introduction An **adjective** is a word that tells something about a noun. When you write, you can use adjectives to help your readers picture what you are describing.

Some adjectives tell *what kind*. They describe how something looks, feels, sounds, tastes, or smells. In the example below, *blue* describes the noun *ocean*. *Cold* describes *water*.

> We swam in the blue ocean.   The water was cold.

Other adjectives tell *how many* there are of something.

> We saw three whales.   There were many dolphins.

What Kind	old, calm, bright, damp, noisy, sour, smoky
How Many	three, twelve, forty, many, several, some

Guided Practice Underline the adjective or adjectives in each sentence. Then draw an arrow from each adjective to the noun that it tells about.

Hint

Sometimes an adjective comes after the noun it describes. When this happens, other words usually come between the noun and adjective.

1 The Davis family goes to a beautiful beach in July.

2 The dunes at the beach are huge.

3 Maddy loves to feel the soft sand between her toes.

4 She likes to jump in the foamy waves.

5 The warm air smells salty from the ocean.

6 Little Chloe digs in the wet sand.

7 Yesterday, she found several shells.

8 Three shells were round.

For numbers 1–3, choose the word in each sentence that is an adjective.

1 The cottage they stay in is two blocks from the ocean.

A two

B cottage

C stay

D ocean

In numbers 4 and 5, what does the adjective in each sentence describe?

2 Father takes the happy children to the beach.

A to

B happy

C beach

D children

4 The hot sand burns in the sun.

A how the sand looks

B how the sand sounds

C how the sand smells

D how the sand feels

3 The children like the smell of the tangy air.

A The

B like

C smell

D tangy

5 The water is salty.

A how the water feels

B how the water looks

C how the water tastes

D how the water sounds

Lesson 5
Adverbs

CCSS
L.3.1a: Explain the function of . . . adverbs in general and their functions in particular sentences.

Introduction An **adverb** is a word that tells something about a verb, or action.

Many adverbs end in *-ly* and tell *how* or *in what way*. When you write, you can use adverbs to help your readers picture clearly what is happening.

The batter quickly ran to first base.   The umpire watched the runner closely.

- The adverb *quickly* describes the verb *ran*. It tells how the batter ran.

- The adverb *closely* describes the verb *watch*. It tells in what way the umpire watched.

Guided Practice Underline the adverb in each sentence. Draw an arrow from the adverb to the verb that it tells about.

Hint

An adverb can come either before or after the verb it describes. A sentence might say *walked slowly,* or it might say *slowly walked*.

1. Jasmine nervously stood at home plate.

2. Her family shouted her name loudly.

3. She carefully rested the bat against her shoulder.

4. The pitcher gripped the ball tightly and then threw it.

5. Jasmine hit the ball sharply, and it soared toward left field.

6. A player tried to catch the ball but accidentally dropped it.

7. Jasmine easily slid into home base.

8. Her whole team cheered wildly!

For numbers 1–3, choose the word in the sentence that is an adverb.

1 The crowd clapped excitedly when Jasmine hit the home run.

A crowd

B clapped

C excitedly

D hit

2 The coach told Jasmine that she had hit the ball perfectly.

A coach

B told

C ball

D perfectly

3 Jasmine's brother waved proudly and jumped from his seat.

A waved

B proudly

C jumped

D seat

For numbers 4 and 5, choose the word that the underlined adverb describes.

4 Jasmine smiled <u>shyly</u> when she saw her family.

A smiled

B saw

C Jasmine

D family

5 She <u>quickly</u> jogged back to the bench and sat down.

A jogged

B back

C bench

D sat

Lesson 6
Plural Nouns

CCSS
L.3.1b: Form and use regular and irregular plural nouns.

Introduction A **singular noun** is a noun that names one person, place, or thing. A **plural noun** names more than one person, place, or thing.

- You can form the plural of most nouns just by adding -*s*.

Singular	a frog	one pond	a turtle
Plural	six frogs	two ponds	some turtles

- To form the plural of a noun that ends in *ch*, *sh*, *ss*, or *x*, add -*es*.
- To form the plural of a noun that ends in a consonant and *y*, change the *y* to *i* and add -*es*.

Singular	bunch	brush	mess	box	fly	baby
Plural	bunches	brushes	messes	boxes	flies	babies

- Some plural nouns do not end in *s*. **Irregular plurals** change in special ways or do not change at all! You just have to remember these plural nouns.

Singular	man	mouse	goose	foot	deer	moose
Plural	men	mice	geese	feet	deer	moose

Guided Practice Write the plural of the noun in parentheses ( ) to complete each sentence.

Hint

If a noun ends in *y* but there is a vowel before the *y*, do not change the *y* to *i*. Just add -*s*.

Example:
boy + **s** = **boys**

1 I went to pick _____ in the woods. (berry)

2 I heard a noise behind some _____. (rock)

3 I thought I would see a few _____. (deer)

4 Then six big birds came out of those _____. (bush)

5 At first I thought they were _____. (goose)

6 Then I realized that they were _____! (turkey)

For numbers 1–3, choose the sentence in which the plural noun or nouns are spelled correctly.

1

A Two familys of mouse live in that stone wall.

B Two familyes of mices live in that stone wall.

C Two family of mouses live in that stone wall.

D Two families of mice live in that stone wall.

2

A Colorful butterflys flit through the air.

B Colorful butterflis flit through the air.

C Colorful butterflies flit through the air.

D Colorful butterflyes flit through the air.

3

A Some mooses drink from the pond.

B Some moose drink from the pond.

C Some moosies drink from the pond.

D Some meese drink from the pond.

For numbers 4 and 5, read each sentence and answer the question.

4 The wind blows through the branchses of the trees.

What is the correct plural of the underlined word?

A branchies

B branchys

C branches

D branchs

5 Are there any bears or foxses in this forest?

What is the correct plural of the underlined word?

A foxs

B foxes

C foxys

D foxies

Introduction You know that a **noun** is a word that names a person, place, or thing.

- Most nouns name things you can see, touch, taste, smell, or hear. These are called **concrete nouns**.

> I love to look at pictures of my father when he was young.

- Some nouns name ideas, feelings, beliefs, or other things that you *cannot* see, touch, taste, smell, or hear. These are called **abstract nouns**.

> My father has many happy memories of his childhood.

Compare these examples of concrete and abstract nouns.

Concrete Nouns	food	hero	prize	seatbelt
Abstract Nouns	hunger	bravery	pride	safety

Guided Practice Circle the abstract noun in each sentence. Then choose one noun you circled, and use it in a sentence about your own family.

Hint

Ask yourself if each word you circled is an idea, a feeling, a belief, or something else that you cannot see, touch, taste, smell, or hear.

1 My grandparents teach us good values.

2 They show their love by giving us big hugs.

3 Grandma reminds us to treat our friends with kindness.

4 Grandpa tells us how important honesty is.

5 I am glad he shares his thoughts with us!

6 _____

_____

For numbers 1–5, choose the abstract noun to complete each sentence.

1 My grandparents came to the United States with _____.

   A dishes

   B suitcases

   C hope

   D maps

2 In the United States, they would find _____.

   A trees

   B baseball

   C subways

   D freedom

3 They wanted their children to have a better _____.

   A house

   B life

   C school

   D car

4 My grandparents needed _____ to move to this country.

   A courage

   B money

   C passports

   D tickets

5 Here, they got lots of _____ from friends and family.

   A rides

   B clothing

   C furniture

   D help

Lesson 8
Simple Verb Tenses

CCSS
L.3.1e: Form and use the simple (e.g., *I walked; I walk; I will walk*) verb tenses.

Introduction The **tense** of a verb helps readers know when something is happening.

- The **present tense** shows that something is happening *now*, or in the present.

  I walk on the grass.

- The **past tense** shows that something happened *before*, or in the past. To form the past tense of most verbs, add *-ed* at the end.

  In 1969, Neil Armstrong walked on the moon.

- The **future tense** shows what *is going to* happen in the future. To form the future tense, put *will* before the verb.

  Maybe someday we will walk on Mars.

Look at the table below. Notice how the verbs change when the tense changes.

Present Tense	look	roam	discover
Past Tense	looked	roamed	discovered
Future Tense	will look	will roam	will discover

Guided Practice **Write the correct tense of the verb to complete each sentence.**

Hint

Words and phrases such as *in 1958*, *today*, and *years from now* can help you decide which verb tense to use.

1 The NASA space program _____ in 1958.
                                          start

2 In 1961, NASA _____ a capsule called *Freedom 7*.
                            launch

3 John Glenn _____ Earth in 1962.
                          orbit

4 Today, astronauts _____ on a space station.
                              stay

5 Years from now, we will _____ to other planets.
                                      travel

For numbers 1–5, choose the sentence in which the tense of the verb is correct.

Answer Form

1 Ⓐ Ⓑ Ⓒ Ⓓ
2 Ⓐ Ⓑ Ⓒ Ⓓ
3 Ⓐ Ⓑ Ⓒ Ⓓ
4 Ⓐ Ⓑ Ⓒ Ⓓ
5 Ⓐ Ⓑ Ⓒ Ⓓ

Number Correct / 5

1

A Our class visited Johnson Space Center next Wednesday.

B Our class will visited Johnson Space Center next Wednesday.

C Our class visit Johnson Space Center next Wednesday.

D Our class will visit Johnson Space Center next Wednesday.

2

A Yesterday we learn about a space rover trip to Mars.

B Yesterday we learned about a space rover trip to Mars.

C Tomorrow we learned about a space rover trip to Mars.

D Yesterday we will learn about a space rover trip to Mars.

3

A The rover, named *Curiosity*, landed on Mars in August of 2012.

B The rover, named *Curiosity*, land on Mars in August of 2012.

C The rover, named *Curiosity*, will land on Mars in August of 2012.

D The rover, named *Curiosity*, will landed on Mars in August of 2012.

4

A Right now, videos from *Curiosity* show the surface of Mars.

B Right now, videos from *Curiosity* will showed the surface of Mars.

C In the future, videos from *Curiosity* showed the surface of Mars.

D In the future, videos from *Curiosity* show the surface of Mars.

5

A At the Space Center next week, I ask more about *Curiosity*.

B At the Space Center next week, I asked more about *Curiosity*.

C At the Space Center next week, I will ask more about *Curiosity*.

D At the Space Center next week, I will asked more about *Curiosity*.

Introduction A verb in the past tense shows that something already happened. Most verbs are **regular verbs**. They each follow the same rules to form the past tense.

- For most regular verbs, add *-ed* to form the past tense.

  watch + **ed**   We watched the dancers on the stage.

- For verbs that end in silent *e*, just add *-d*.

  move + **d**   They moved gracefully across the floor.

- For verbs that end in a consonant and *y*, change the *y* to *i* before you add *-ed*.

  carry – **y** + **i** + **ed**   One dancer carried the other.

- For verbs that end in a short vowel sound and a consonant, double the consonant before you add *-ed*.

  flip + **p** + **ed**   Then he flipped her in the air!

Guided Practice **Write the past tense of the verb to complete each sentence. Be sure to use correct spelling.**

Hint

If a verb ends in *y* but there is a vowel before the *y*, do <u>not</u> change the *y* to *i*. Just add *-ed*.

Example:
stay + **ed** = **stayed**

1 Yuki _____ in a dance show last night.
        perform

2 The dancers _____ to several different songs.
              dance

3 They _____ to the music.
        sway

4 Near the end, the music suddenly _____.
                        stop

5 Yuki's teacher _____ to fix behind the stage.
              hurry

For numbers 1–5, choose the correct spelling of the past tense verb to complete each sentence.

1 My school _____ a talent show last week.

   A presentd

   B presented

   C presentted

   D present

2 I _____ my act every day for a month.

   A practicied

   B practiceed

   C practice

   D practiced

3 I _____ that I would make a mistake.

   A worreid

   B worryd

   C worried

   D worryed

4 For my act, I _____ four tomatoes.

   A juggled

   B juggleed

   C jugglled

   D juggld

5 The audience _____ loudly when I was done.

   A claped

   B clappd

   C clapped

   D clapedd

Lesson 10
Irregular Verbs

CCSS
L.3.1d: Form and use . . . irregular verbs.

Introduction Most verbs are regular. Regular verbs end in -*ed* when they show that something happened in the past. Some verbs are irregular. **Irregular verbs** change in special ways to show past time.

Present	Sometimes I make my own lunch.
Past	Yesterday I made a sandwich.

Another way to tell about the past is to use the helping verb *has, have,* or *had* with the past form of the main verb. Some irregular verbs change spelling when they are used with *has, have,* or *had*.

Present	Past	Past with *Has, Have,* or *Had*
begin	began	(has, have, had) begun
come	came	(has, have, had) come
eat	ate	(has, have, had) eaten
go	went	(has, have, had) gone
make	made	(has, have, had) made
see	saw	(has, have, had) seen
run	ran	(has, have, had) run
give	gave	(has, have, had) given

Guided Practice **Circle the form of the verb that correctly completes each sentence.**

Hint

To know which past form of the verb to use, look for the helping verb *has, have,* or *had.* Sometimes the word *not* or another word comes between the helping verb and the main verb.

1 I have always _____ each day with a healthy breakfast.

    begun   **began**   **begin**

2 Yesterday Mom _____ me a bowl of oatmeal with fruit.

    given   **give**   **gave**

3 My dad has _____ yummy banana bread.

    made   **maked**   **make**

4 Grandma had not _____ yet, so she had some, too.

    eaten   **eat**   **ate**

For numbers 1–5, read each sentence. Then choose the word that replaces the underlined verb and makes the sentence correct.

1 Mom and I <u>go</u> to the store last week.

A gone

B goed

C went

D goned

2 We had <u>ran</u> out of healthy snacks.

A run

B runned

C ranned

D rund

3 At the store, we <u>see</u> a lot of cookies and candy.

A seen

B seened

C sawed

D saw

4 Mom has never <u>give</u> me snacks like those.

A gave

B gaven

C given

D gived

5 We <u>come</u> home with carrots and raisins.

A camed

B came

C camen

D comed

Lesson 11
Subject–Verb Agreement

CCSS
L.3.1f: Ensure subject–verb . . . agreement.

Introduction The **subject** of a sentence tells whom or what the sentence is about. A subject can tell about one or more than one person, place, or thing. The verb in the sentence must **agree** with, or match in number, the subject. The subject can be singular or plural.

Singular	Plural
subject verb	**subject verb**
Kenji writes poems for a hobby.	His brothers write songs.

Follow these rules if the subject is a singular noun or the pronoun *he*, *she*, or *it*.

Add -*s* to the end of most verbs.	Tara collects old trains.
Add -*es* if the verb ends in *ch*, *sh*, *ss*, or *x*.	She washes the trains.
Change *y* to *i* before adding -*es* if the verb ends in a consonant and *y*.	She tries to fix them.

Do <u>not</u> add anything to the verb if the subject is a plural noun or the pronoun *I*, *you*, *we*, or *they*.

Sometimes I help Tara, too. The trains always look beautiful.

Guided Practice **Cross out each verb that does not agree with its subject. Write the verb correctly above it.**

Hint

If a verb ends in a vowel and *y*, just add -*s* if the subject is singular. Do <u>not</u> add anything if the subject is plural.

Example:
Tina **plays** sports.
We **play**, too.

Many people enjoys hobbies. My friend Simon likes baseball

cards. He keep them in a huge box. My sister Kim watch cartoons.

Then she draws her favorite characters. My grandparents travel a lot.

They saves coins from everywhere. Even our dog finds bones and

bury them in our yard.

For numbers 1–5, read each sentence. Then choose the correct verb to agree with the subject.

1 My uncle _____ for a hobby.

   A fishs

   B fishies

   C fishes

   D fish

2 He _____ the fish home in a pail.

   A carrys

   B carries

   C carryes

   D carry

3 My sisters _____ to hike.

   A likes

   B likse

   C liks

   D like

4 They _____ for interesting flowers and rocks.

   A searchs

   B searches

   C search

   D searchse

5 Dora _____ the names of many rocks.

   A knows

   B knowes

   C knowz

   D know

Lesson 12
Pronoun–Antecedent Agreement

CCSS
L.3.1f: Ensure . . . pronoun–antecedent agreement.

👥 Introduction You know that pronouns take the place of nouns. Pronouns must **agree** with, or match in number, the noun they replace. The singular pronouns are *I, you, he, she, it, me, him,* and *her.* The plural pronouns are *we, you, they, us,* and *them.*

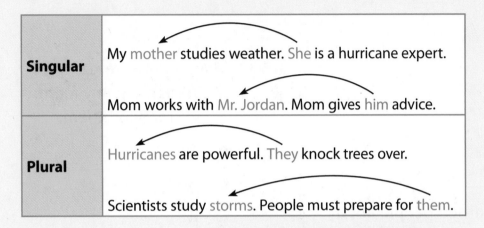

Singular	My mother studies weather. She is a hurricane expert. Mom works with Mr. Jordan. Mom gives him advice.
Plural	Hurricanes are powerful. They knock trees over. Scientists study storms. People must prepare for them.

👥 Guided Practice **Cross out each pronoun that does not agree with the noun it replaces. Write the correct pronoun above it.**

Hint

Use *he* or *him* when you are talking about a boy or a man. Use *she* or *her* when you are talking about a girl or a woman.

1 The weather interests Sara. Mom teaches him about it.

2 Mom knows about storms. She keeps track of it.

3 Grandpa remembers a bad storm. He tells about them.

4 The wind was 95 miles an hour. She was very strong.

5 Trees crashed down. It fell on the house.

6 Grandpa was on the porch. They yelled for Grandma.

7 Grandma heard Grandpa. She ran outside to find them.

8 My grandparents were safe. It stayed in a shelter.

For numbers 1–5, read each sentence. Then choose the pronoun that agrees with the underlined noun.

1 <u>Mr. Jordan</u> reports the weather. _____ gets help from my mother.

A She

B He

C It

D They

2 Mr. Jordan warned <u>people</u> about a hurricane and told _____ what to do.

A him

B her

C them

D it

3 <u>People</u> stayed safe because _____ listened to his advice.

A she

B he

C it

D they

4 <u>Mayor Maria Perez</u> called Mr. Jordan and my mom. _____ thanked them.

A She

B He

C It

D We

5 My mom enjoys working with <u>Mr. Jordan</u>. She has a lot of respect for _____.

A she

B he

C her

D him

Lesson 13
Comparative and Superlative Adjectives and Adverbs

CCSS
L.3.1g: Form and use comparative and superlative adjectives and adverbs, and choose between them depending on what is to be modified.

Introduction When you write, you can use adjectives and adverbs to tell how things are alike or different.

- Add *-er* to most adjectives to compare two people, places, or things.
  Add *-est* to compare three or more people, places, or things.

cold + **er**	The lake is colder than the pond.
cold + **est**	Of all bodies of water, the ocean is the coldest place to swim.

- Use *more* with adverbs that end in *-ly* to compare two actions.
  Use *most* to compare three or more actions.

more + gracefully	Emma swims more gracefully than Madison.
most + gracefully	Ann swims the most gracefully of all the girls.

Guided Practice **Read each sentence. Circle the correct word or words to complete it.**

Hint

Never use *more* or *most* together with adjectives that end in *-er* or *-est*.

Correct:
fuller, fullest
Incorrect:
more fuller,
most fullest

1 The adults' pool is _____ than the children's pool.

   deepest   deeper   more deeply

2 My little brother swims _____ than I do.

   slowly   more slowly   slowest

3 The morning is the _____ time of all at the pool.

   most calmest   more calm   calmest

4 This lifeguard blows her whistle the _____ of all the guards.

   most loudly   louder   more louder

For numbers 1–5, choose the correct word or words to complete each sentence.

1 Nikki built the _____ sand castle on the beach.

- **A** tall
- **B** most tallest
- **C** more tall
- **D** tallest

2 I saw a seahorse that was _____ than my fingernail.

- **A** most small
- **B** more smaller
- **C** smaller
- **D** smallest

3 Dan put on his snorkel _____ than his little brother did.

- **A** most carefully
- **B** more carefully
- **C** careful
- **D** carefully

4 Pari was the _____ swimmer of all of us.

- **A** stronger
- **B** strongest
- **C** more stronger
- **D** most strongest

5 Max held the little crab the _____of all the children.

- **A** most gently
- **B** gentle
- **C** more gently
- **D** gently

Introduction   A **conjunction** is a word that is used to join other words, groups of words, or sentences. The words *and*, *but*, *or*, and *so* are conjunctions.

- Use *and* when you mean "also."

  Birds and dogs are my favorite animals.

- Use *but* when you want to show a difference.

  Mario's cat is playful, but Lila's cat likes to sleep.

- Use *or* when you want to show a choice.

  Dad says we can have a kitten or a puppy.

- Use *so* when you want to give a reason.

  I love animals, so I like having a lot of pets.

Guided Practice   **Write the conjunction *and*, *but*, *or*, or *so* to complete each sentence.**

Hint

Sometimes more than one conjunction can make sense in a sentence. Choose the conjunction that makes the meaning clearest.

1 Poodles _____ collies are both smart dogs.

2 I take my dog to the park, _____ he can get more exercise.

3 Shanti likes cats _____ not dogs.

4 Pedro wants a dog, _____ he does not want a big dog.

5 Kim walks her dog _____ then feeds him.

6 Should we name the puppy Ernie _____ Bert?

7 Our dog doesn't obey, _____ we need to send him to a dog trainer.

8 Pedro might get a dog today, _____ he will wait until tomorrow.

For numbers 1–5, choose the best conjunction to complete each sentence.

1 Parrots are colorful _____ smart birds.

A and

B but

C or

D so

2 Most parrots live in jungles, _____ some of them live in homes as pets.

A and

B but

C or

D so

3 Parrots have strong, curved beaks, _____ they can crack open seeds.

A and

B but

C or

D so

4 Anisa wants a parrot _____ no pet at all.

A and

B but

C or

D so

5 I would like to have both a parrot _____ a parakeet.

A and

B but

C or

D so

Lesson 15
Simple and Compound Sentences

CCSS
L.3.1h: Use coordinating . . . conjunctions.
L.3.1i: Produce . . . compound . . . sentences.

 Introduction A **sentence** is a group of words that tells a complete thought.

- A **simple sentence** has one subject and one predicate. The **subject** tells whom or what the sentence is about. The **predicate** tells what the subject does or is.

subject   predicate
[Alfredo] [goes to art class on Tuesday and Thursday.]

- A **compound sentence** has two simple sentences joined together by the conjunction *and*, *but*, *or*, or *so*. There is usually a comma before the conjunction.

simple sentence   simple sentence
[Alfredo likes art class], but [his sister enjoys music class.]

- Combining two short sentences into a compound sentence can make your writing less choppy. It also helps you show that two ideas are connected.

Alfredo painted a picture. His sister sang a song.

Alfredo painted a picture, and his sister sang a song.

Guided Practice Combine each pair of simple sentences to make a compound sentence. Use the conjunction in parentheses ( ).

Hint

Be sure to put a comma before the conjunction in each compound sentence you write.

1 Should we start class? Should we wait? (or)

_____

2 I finished my picture. Neil did not finish his. (but)

_____

3 Liz has a flute lesson soon. She must practice. (so)

_____

4 She made up a song. It sounded great! (and)

_____

For numbers 1–4, pick the choice that correctly combines the two simple sentences into a compound sentence.

Answer Form
1 Ⓐ Ⓑ Ⓒ Ⓓ
2 Ⓐ Ⓑ Ⓒ Ⓓ
3 Ⓐ Ⓑ Ⓒ Ⓓ
4 Ⓐ Ⓑ Ⓒ Ⓓ

Number Correct /4

1 Mr. Ramirez loves music. He is a great teacher.

A Mr. Ramirez loves music and he is a great teacher.

B Mr. Ramirez loves music, but he is a great teacher.

C Mr. Ramirez loves music, and he is a great teacher.

D Mr. Ramirez loves music, or he is a great teacher.

2 Anita was going to sing. She had a sore throat.

A Anita was going to sing, but she had a sore throat.

B Anita was going to sing, so she had a sore throat.

C Anita was going to sing, or she had a sore throat.

D Anita was going to sing, and she had a sore throat.

3 You may play the piano first. You may play the drums first.

A You may play the piano first, and you may play the drums first.

B You may play the piano first, so you may play the drums first.

C You may play the piano first, but you may play the drums first.

D You may play the piano first, or you may play the drums first.

4 We cannot hear the music. Please make it louder.

A We cannot hear the music, and please make it louder.

B We cannot hear the music, so please make it louder.

C We cannot hear the music, but please make it louder.

D We cannot hear the music so, please make it louder.

Lesson 16
Subordinating Conjunctions and Complex Sentences

CCSS
L.3.1h: Use . . . subordinating conjunctions.
L.3.1i: Produce . . . complex sentences.

Introduction Simple sentences can be combined using different kinds of conjunctions.

- One way to combine simple sentences is to use a conjunction such as *after*, *because*, *when*, or *while*. When you combine two simple sentences with such conjunctions, you form a **complex sentence**.

simple sentence		simple sentence
[Yasmin did not stay for the game]	although	[she loves soccer.]

- In a complex sentence, the conjunction shows how the ideas in the two simple sentences go together.

- The conjunction can come at the beginning or in the middle of the sentence.

Conjunctions	When to Use	Examples
because	to explain or give a reason	Yasmin went home because she felt ill.
after, before, until, when, while	to show when things happen	She had a snack before she took a nap.
		When she woke up, she watched TV.
although, unless	to compare or to show an exception	She'll stay home Monday unless she feels better.

Guided Practice Combine each pair of simple sentences to make a complex sentence. Use the conjunction in parentheses ( ).

Hint

When you begin a sentence with a conjunction, use a comma after the first simple sentence.

Example:
Before you play soccer, you should stretch.

1 The soccer players have fun. They practice. (while)

_____

2 Kayla works hard. She wants to be a better player. (because)

_____

3 Milo was on the team. He got hurt. (until)

_____

For numbers 1–4, first read the simple sentences. Then pick the choice that correctly combines the simple sentences into a complex sentence.

1 The game had already begun. We arrived.

 A The game had already begun because we arrived.

 B Although the game had already begun, we arrived.

 C The game had already begun when we arrived.

 D The game had already begun while we arrived.

2 It started to rain. The game was not called off.

 A Although it started to rain, the game was not called off.

 B Because it started to rain, the game was not called off.

 C It started to rain when the game was not called off.

 D It started to rain unless the game was not called off.

3 The Hawks won. They scored the most goals.

 A The Hawks won unless they scored the most goals.

 B The Hawks won before they scored the most goals.

 C After the Hawks won, they scored the most goals.

 D The Hawks won because they scored the most goals.

4 The game was over. We went out for pizza.

 A Until the game was over, we went out for pizza.

 B After the game was over, we went out for pizza.

 C The game was over unless we went out for pizza.

 D The game was over because we went out for pizza.

👥 **Introduction** There is a special way to write the title of a book, magazine, newspaper, or movie.

- Always capitalize the first word, the last word, and all the important words in a title.
- Do not capitalize short words such as *a, an, the, and, of, for, in,* and *on* unless they are the first or last word of the title.

Book	*The Adventures of Peter Vine*
Magazine	*Fun for You and Me*
Newspaper	*The Daily News*
Movie	*Sara Drake and the Secret Cave*

👥 **Guided Practice** **Write each title correctly, adding capital letters where they are needed.**

Hint

Usually the title of a book, magazine, newspaper, or movie is shown in *italics*. But when you write one of these titles by hand, you should underline it instead.

1. *oliver in space* (movie)

2. *abby and the zebra* (book)

3. *explore and more* (magazine)

4. *the star county times* (newspaper)

5. *a dragon in town* (movie)

6. *lily the lucky ladybug* (book)

7. *diary of an amazing mouse* (movie)

8. *sports for healthy kids* (magazine)

1 _____

2 _____

3 _____

4 _____

5 _____

6 _____

7 _____

8 _____

275

For numbers 1–5, choose the correct answer to each question.

1 How should the title of this movie be written?

A *a Hog on a Log*

B *A Hog On a Log*

C *a Hog on a log*

D *A Hog on a Log*

2 How should the title of this book be written?

A *Sam The Storm chaser*

B *Sam the Storm Chaser*

C *Sam the storm Chaser*

D *Sam The Storm Chaser*

3 How should the title of this magazine be written?

A *The Planets And The Stars*

B *The planets and the Stars*

C *The Planets and the Stars*

D *the Planets And the Stars*

4 How should the title of this newspaper be written?

A *Weekly News for All*

B *Weekly News For all*

C *Weekly news for All*

D *Weekly news For all*

5 How should the title of this book be written?

A *And the Cat Wants in*

B *And the Cat Wants In*

C *and the Cat Wants in*

D *And The Cat Wants In*

Introduction What is the name of the street where your school is? What city or town is it in? What is the name of the state where you live? When you put all of this information together, you get an **address**.

When you write an address, place a **comma (,)** between the name of the street and the city. Place another comma between the name of the city and the state.

> The store is at 300 Craig Street, Durham, North Carolina.

Guided Practice Rewrite each address. Add commas where they are needed. Then finish the last sentence by writing your own address.

Hint

The name of a street can also have the word *Road*, *Drive*, *Lane*, or *Avenue* at the end. The comma always comes after those words.

1 18 West Lane Orlando Florida

_____

2 2 Griggs Avenue Albany New York

_____

3 531 Front Street Monroe Wisconsin

_____

4 1538 Oakwood Drive Canton Ohio

_____

5 49 Jeffrey Road Athens Georgia

_____

6 My address is _____

_____

_____

For numbers 1–4, pick the choice that correctly punctuates the address underlined in the sentence.

1 My grandmother lives at <u>945 Peters Street Fresno California</u>.

   A 945 Peters, Street Fresno, California

   B 945 Peters Street, Fresno, California

   C 945 Peters Street Fresno, California

   D 945 Peters Street, Fresno California

2 I sent the card to <u>310 Medford Road Concord North Carolina</u>.

   A 310 Medford Road, Concord, North Carolina

   B 310, Medford Road, Concord, North Carolina

   C 310 Medford Road, Concord North, Carolina

   D 310 Medford Road Concord, North Carolina

3 The address on the envelope was <u>18 Arcola Lane Tucson Arizona</u>.

   A 18 Arcola, Lane, Tucson, Arizona

   B 18 Arcola Lane, Tucson Arizona

   C 18 Arcola Lane, Tucson, Arizona

   D 18 Arcola Lane Tucson, Arizona

4 Hiro's family moved to <u>4 Charles Drive Bristol Rhode Island</u>.

   A 4 Charles Drive Bristol, Rhode Island

   B 4 Charles Drive, Bristol Rhode Island

   C 4, Charles Drive, Bristol, Rhode Island

   D 4 Charles Drive, Bristol, Rhode Island

Punctuating Dialogue

CCSS
L.3.2c: Use commas and quotation marks in dialogue.

Introduction When characters in a story talk to each other, this is a **dialogue**. When you write a dialogue, use **quotation marks** (" ") before and after each speaker's words.

> Mr. Simons said, "We're going on a field trip!"
> "Hooray!" the class shouted.

When a speaker's words come last in a sentence, use a **comma (,)** to separate the speaker's words from the rest of the sentence.

> Myra asked, "Where are we going?"
> Mr. Simons answered, "We are going to the Natural History Museum."

Guided Practice **Read each sentence. Then rewrite the sentence on the line below, adding quotation marks and commas where needed.**

Hint

The end punctuation after a speaker's words should be *inside* the quotation marks.

Correct: "It's a dog, isn't it?"

Incorrect: "It's a dog, isn't it"?

1 I am so excited about our trip to the museum! Janie said.

_____

_____

2 Carlos asked Do you think it will be boring?

_____

_____

3 Then Justin explained It's a chance to go someplace new.

_____

_____

4 I think we'll have a great time! Tanisha added.

_____

_____

For numbers 1–5, choose the sentence in each group that uses correct punctuation.

1
  A "This museum is gigantic"! Anna exclaimed.

  B "This museum is gigantic!" Anna exclaimed.

  C "This museum is gigantic! Anna exclaimed."

  D This museum is gigantic! "Anna exclaimed."

2
  A Celia said, "Everyone should visit this museum."

  B Celia said "Everyone should visit this museum."

  C Celia said, Everyone should visit this museum.

  D "Celia said" Everyone should visit this museum.

3
  A Alberto asked. "What is this?"

  B Alberto asked, "What is this"?

  C Alberto asked "What is this"!

  D Alberto asked, "What is this?"

4
  A I've never seen anything like it! Juanita replied.

  B I've never seen anything like it! "Juanita replied."

  C "I've never seen anything like it!" Juanita replied.

  D "I've never seen anything like it! Juanita replied."

5
  A Billy announced, "It's a fossil footprint."

  B Billy announced. "It's a fossil footprint."

  C Billy announced "It's a fossil footprint".

  D "Billy announced, "It's a fossil footprint.

Possessive Nouns

CCSS
L.3.2d: Form and use possessives.

Introduction Some nouns show that a person or animal owns something. A noun that shows ownership is called a **possessive noun**. For example, *the girl's hat* means that the girl owns or has the hat. *The tiger's fur* means that the fur belongs to the tiger.

- To form the possessive of a singular noun, add an **apostrophe (')** and then an *-s*.

seller + 's	The ticket seller's booth is at the front of the zoo.

- To form the possessive of a plural noun, add an apostrophe (') *after* the *-s*.

lions + '	The lions' area is near the back of the zoo.

Guided Practice **Write the possessive form of the noun in parentheses ( ) to complete each phrase.**

Hint

How can you tell if the possessive noun should be singular or plural? Look at the ending of the noun in ( ). Also look for clue words, such as *a, one, several,* and *few*.

1 a _____ key (zookeeper)

2 several _____ ears (bunnies)

3 one _____ flippers (penguin)

4 a few _____ tails (foxes)

5 three _____ brooms (cleaners)

6 a _____ tickets (guest)

7 some _____ nests (cranes)

8 an _____ egg (emu)

For numbers 1–5, choose the correct way to write each underlined noun.

1 Several <u>workers</u> pails had food for the animals.

   A worker's'

   B workers

   C worker's

   D workers'

2 The workers put bottles in a few <u>babies</u> mouths.

   A babies'

   B babie's'

   C babies

   D babie's

3 The zookeeper pointed out three <u>ostriches</u> strong legs.

   A ostriche's's

   B ostriches

   C ostriches'

   D ostriche's

4 There was a big spray of water from an <u>elephants</u> trunk.

   A elephants

   B elephant's

   C elephants's

   D elephants'

5 We loved seeing one <u>peacocks</u> colorful feathers.

   A parrots'

   B parrots

   C parrot's

   D parrots's

Lesson 21
Possessive Pronouns

CCSS
L.3.1f: Ensure . . . pronoun–antecedent agreement.
L.3.2d: Form and use possessives.

Introduction You know that a possessive noun shows ownership. When a pronoun shows ownership, it is called a **possessive pronoun**.

- A possessive pronoun can take the place of a possessive noun.

> **Her**
> Lena had the idea for the bake sale. ~~Lena's~~ aunt made bread.

- A possessive pronoun can be singular or plural. It must agree with, or match, the noun it is replacing.

	Possessive Pronouns	Examples
Singular	my, your, his, her, its	Brett and his sister baked cakes.
Plural	your, our, their	The twins and their dad helped.

Guided Practice **Write a possessive pronoun to take the place of the underlined word or words.**

Hint

The possessive pronoun *their* means "belonging to them." Use it when you want to show that two or more people own or have something.

1 Maria's colorful signs : _____ colorful signs

2 the tray's handles : _____ handles

3 Tim's and Lena's brownies : _____ brownies

4 Michael's yummy churros : _____ yummy churros

5 Pedro's and my cupcakes : _____ cupcakes

6 the bagel that belongs to you : _____ bagel

7 the basket that is mine : _____ basket

8 the pan that belongs to the two of you : _____ pan

For numbers 1–5, choose the pronoun that correctly completes the sentence by agreeing with the underlined word or words.

1 <u>Mr. Blanco</u> asked _____ son to set up the food tables.

A his

B her

C our

D its

2 <u>One table</u> was broken, so Jim fixed _____ wobbly legs.

A her

B our

C its

D their

3 <u>Mrs. Chin</u> put _____ punch bowl on the table.

A his

B her

C its

D their

4 <u>Sari and Lil</u> sold _____ tasty cookies right away.

A her

B its

C his

D their

5 <u>My dad and I</u> were proud of _____ healthy snacks.

A your

B our

C her

D their

Lesson 22
Adding Suffixes

CCSS
L.3.2e: Use conventional spelling for . . . adding suffixes to base words (e.g., *sitting, smiled, cries, happiness*).

Introduction A **suffix** is a word part added to the end of a base word. Adding a suffix changes the meaning of a word.

base word	suffix
walk	+ **ing** = walking

Follow these spelling rules when adding suffixes to base words.

When a Suffix Begins with a Vowel	
If the base word ends in a short vowel sound and one consonant, double the consonant.	b**at** + **t** + ing = batting j**og** + **g** + ed = jogged
If the base word ends in a silent -*e*, drop the *e*.	smil**e** – **e** + ing = smiling saf**e** – **e** + er = safer
When a Base Word Ends with a Consonant and *y*	
Change the *y* to *i* before adding most suffixes.	hap**py** – **y** + **i** + ness = happiness sil**ly** – **y** + **i** + est = silliest

Guided Practice Add the suffix shown to each word. Write the new word.

Hint

When you add -*ing* to a verb that ends in *y*, do not change the *y* to *i*.

Example:
try + **ing** = **trying**
fly + **ing** = **flying**

1 hike + ed _____

2 skip + ing _____

3 nice + er _____

4 hurry + ing _____

5 silly + ness _____

6 try + ed _____

7 dive + ing _____

8 funny + est _____

For numbers 1–5, read each question and choose the correct answer.

1 How would you spell the new word if you added the suffix *-ing* to "spin"?

A spineing

B spining

C spinning

D spinneing

2 How would you spell the new word if you added the suffix *-er* to "brave"?

A braveer

B bravver

C bravr

D braver

3 How would you spell the new word if you added the suffix *-ness* to "heavy"?

A heavyness

B heaviness

C heavyiness

D heavieness

4 How would you spell the new word if you added the suffix *-ed* to "smile"?

A smiled

B smield

C smild

D smilled

5 How would you spell the new word if you added the suffix *-est* to "rainy"?

A rainyest

B rainyiest

C rainest

D rainiest

Lesson 23
Using Reference Works

CCSS
L.3.2g: Consult reference materials, including beginning dictionaries, as needed to check and correct spellings.

👥 **Introduction** What can you do if you aren't sure how to spell a word? A **dictionary** is a good place to look to find the correct spelling of an unfamiliar word.

- A dictionary lists words in alphabetical order. Each entry shows a word's pronunciation, part of speech, and meaning.
- **Guide words** at the top of each page show the first and last entry words on the page.

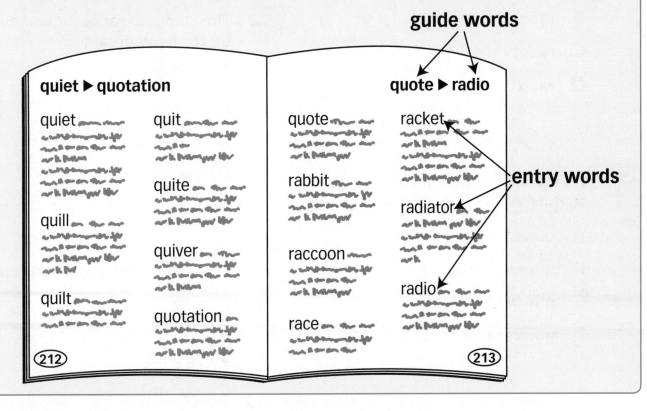

guide words

quiet ▶ quotation

quote ▶ radio

quiet

quit

quill

quite

quilt

quiver

quotation

quote

rabbit

raccoon

race

racket

radiator

radio

entry words

212

213

👥 **Guided Practice** **Use a dictionary to check the spelling of each underlined word. If the word is spelled wrong, write the correct spelling.**

Hint

Read the guide words at the top of the dictionary page to decide if the word you are looking for is on that page.

1 Do you <u>rememmber</u> your dreams? _____

2 <u>Sometims</u> dreams are funny. _____

3 Some dreams can be <u>scary</u>. _____

4 I had a <u>wierd</u> dream yesterday. _____

For numbers 1–5, read each sentence. Then use the sample dictionary on page 45 to choose the correct spelling of the underlined word.

1 Last night a <u>rabit</u> hopped into my bedroom.

  A rabbet

  B rabbit

  C rabet

  D rabit

2 He sat still, but his whiskers began to <u>quivver</u>.

  A quiver

  B quivur

  C quivure

  D quivver

3 He said, "I must hide from a <u>racoon</u>!"

  A racoonn

  B raccon

  C racon

  D raccoon

4 The clanging <u>radeator</u> woke me up from my dream.

  A radeator

  B radeatur

  C radiator

  D radiatur

5 All of that clanging made quite a <u>rackit</u>.

  A rackitt

  B rackett

  C racket

  D raccket

Choosing Words and Phrases for Effect

CCSS
L.3.3a: Choose words and phrases for effect.

Introduction When writing, pick words and phrases that express your ideas and experiences in a lively, interesting way.

- Replace general words or phrases with more precise words or phrases.

  On Saturday
  ~~Last week~~ I went to a nice swimming party.

- Swap general verbs with more specific or descriptive verbs.

  attended
  On Saturday I ~~went to~~ a nice swimming party.

- Trade in weak adjectives for stronger or more interesting adjectives.

  an amazing
  On Saturday I attended ~~a nice~~ swimming party.

- The final sentence is much more precise and interesting to read than the first one.

  On Saturday I attended an amazing swimming party.

Guided Practice **Circle the word or phrase that can best take the place of the underlined word or phrase. The goal is to make each sentence more precise and interesting.**

Hint

When replacing a word or phrase, make sure you are changing the effect of the sentence but not its meaning.

1 The swimming party started in the <u>afternoon</u>.

    at noon   **later on**   **early**

2 When I arrived, the sun <u>was</u> over the pool.

    rose   **moved**   **blazed**

3 Everyone at the party was <u>very glad</u> to swim.

    ready   **surprised**   **excited**

4 The pool <u>was</u> a depth of 12 feet.

    measured   **seemed**   **had**

5 I walked to the edge and slowly <u>got</u> into the pool.

    went   **jumped**   **eased**

For numbers 1–5, which word or phrase would replace the underlined words with more specific language? (The correct answer will not change the meaning of the sentence.)

1 At the pool party there was <u>good-tasting</u> food such as pizza.

   A delicious

   B salty

   C filling

   D cheap

2 I ate <u>a lot of</u> pizza.

   A some

   B a piece of

   C a few bites of

   D at least five slices of

3 Then I noticed that someone had brought <u>a dog</u> to the pool.

   A an animal

   B a golden retriever

   C a pet

   D a creature

4 A sign next to the pool <u>said</u> that pets were not allowed.

   A decided

   B wondered

   C warned

   D thought

5 The dog was <u>nice</u>, so the pool manager let it stay.

   A friendly

   B small

   C huge

   D smart

Lesson 25
Spoken and Written English

CCSS

L.3.3b: Recognize and observe differences between the conventions of spoken and written standard English.

Introduction When you speak with friends, you don't have to worry about every word and how it sounds. But when you write, you want your words to be exact and clear.

- When you speak, you often use single words and phrases. When you write, you should use complete sentences.

Spoken English	Written English
Dan: Want to see the stars tonight? **Ava:** Nah. Too many clouds. Maybe tomorrow.	Clear nights are the best time to see stars.

- When you speak, you often use slang such as *hey* or *can't*. When you write, you usually do not use slang or contractions.

Spoken English	Written English
Dan: That's a shooting star. **Ava:** Hey, there's another one. Whoa! There are so many I can't count them all!	During the meteor shower, more than 150 shooting stars came streaking across the sky.

Guided Practice Read each sentence with a partner. Which ones sound like spoken language? Write *spoken* or *written* next to each sentence. Tell your partner which clues helped you decide.

Hint

To find spoken language, look for slang such as *yup* and *awesome*. Also, look for sentences that are not complete.

1 This is okay homework. _____

2 Yup, really good. _____

3 Learning about meteors is interesting. _____

4 The next meteor shower will be in August. _____

5 Awesome. Can't wait! _____

6 The number of shooting stars people see depends on where they stand. _____

Dan and Ava are watching the sky again. Read what they say in numbers 1–4. Then rewrite the information as if it were a report about stars.

1 **Ava:** Stars are really cool, and constellations are even cooler.

Dan: Right, they look like pictures of things.

_____

_____

2 **Ava:** Wow! That's the Big Dipper. Looks like a ladle. See its handle?

Dan: Yeah, I see it. I can count all seven stars.

_____

_____

3 **Ava:** Check out the North Star. It's in the Little Dipper.

Dan: Ever get lost? The North Star can help you find your way.

_____

_____

4 **Ava:** What are those bright stars? The ones over there.

Dan: Don't know their names. They're part of another constellation.

_____

_____

Lesson 26
Using Context Clues

CCSS
L.3.4a: Use sentence-level context as a clue to the meaning of a word or phrase.

Introduction Sometimes when you read, you will see a word you do not know. You can figure out its meaning by looking at the words around it. You can use **context clues**.

- Sometimes a sentence includes a definition of the word.

> **definition**
> Living in a frigid, or **extremely cold**, place can be difficult.

- A sentence might also give an example that explains a word.

> **example**
> Frigid temperatures in the Arctic can be as low as **58°F below zero**.

Guided Practice **Use context clues to figure out the meaning of each underlined word. Write the meaning. Then circle the words that were a clue.**

Hint

As you read, look for the words *such as*. These words might introduce an example that helps you figure out the meaning of an unknown word.

1 Animals <u>adapt</u> by changing in a way that allows them to live in a certain place.

2 The polar bear's furry snout and ears help it <u>survive</u>, or stay alive, in the cold Arctic.

3 The white fur of the Arctic fox lets it hide from <u>predators</u> such as wolves.

4 The Arctic bee has to <u>shiver</u>, or shake, to keep itself warm.

1 _____

2 _____

3 _____

4 _____

Read the sentence below. Then use it to answer numbers 1 and 2.

The ground squirrel <u>hibernates</u>, sleeping for months during the winter.

1 What does the word <u>hibernates</u> mean?

A hides in the ground

B hides for a long, long time

C sleeps because it has nowhere to go

D sleeps to live through low temperatures

2 What words help you understand the meaning of <u>hibernates</u>?

A "ground" and "squirrel"

B "ground squirrel" and "months"

C "sleeping" and "during the winter"

D "months" and "winter"

Read the sentence below. Then use it to answer numbers 3 and 4.

The fur on polar bears helps them <u>repel</u>, or keep away, cold water.

3 What does the word <u>repel</u> mean?

A to fight

B to push something away

C to make something warm

D to soak up or take in

4 What words help you understand the meaning of <u>repel</u>?

A "keep away"

B "fur on polar bears"

C "cold water"

D "helps them"

Lesson 27
Prefixes and Suffixes

CCSS

L.3.4b: Determine the meaning of the new word formed when a known affix is added to a known word (e.g., *agreeable/disagreeable, comfortable/uncomfortable, care/careless, heat/preheat*).

Introduction Use your knowledge of word parts to figure out what new words mean.

- A **prefix** is a word part added to the beginning of a word. Adding a prefix changes the meaning of a base word.

Prefix	Meaning	Example	Meaning
dis-	"not" or "opposite of"	dislike	"to not like"
pre-	"before"	prewash	"to wash before"
un-	"not" or "opposite of"	untrue	"not true"

- A **suffix** is a word part added to the end of a word. Adding a suffix changes the meaning of a base word.

Suffix	Meaning	Example	Meaning
-able	"can be" or "able to"	trainable	"can be trained"
-ful	"full of" or "having"	skillful	"having skill"
-less	"without"	useless	"without use"

- Some words have both a prefix and a suffix: <u>un</u>comfort<u>able</u>, <u>dis</u>agree<u>able</u>.

Guided Practice **Write the base word and the prefix or suffix that make up each underlined word. Then tell a partner what the underlined word means.**

Hint

A prefix or a suffix can have more than one meaning. Think about which meaning makes sense in the sentence.

1 Here are some ways to be <u>helpful</u> at home.

helpful = _____ + _____
　　　　　　　base word　　　　**suffix**

2 Try to be <u>agreeable</u> with your family.

agreeable = _____ + _____
　　　　　　　base word　　　　**suffix**

3 Never be <u>dishonest</u>.

dishonest = _____ + _____
　　　　　　　prefix　　　　**base word**

4 Try to share, and never be <u>unfair</u>.

unfair = _____ + _____
　　　　　　prefix　　　　**base word**

For numbers 1–5, read each sentence. Then choose the correct meaning of each underlined word.

1 Follow these <u>useful</u> safety tips.

   A without use

   B not used

   C having use

   D before using

2 Don't be <u>careless</u> when you carry something hot.

   A without care

   B full of care

   C able to care

   D having care

3 Let adults <u>preview</u> movies you want to see.

   A not view

   B view without you

   C mostly view

   D view before

4 Never <u>unbuckle</u> your seatbelt while in a moving car.

   A buckle before

   B do the opposite of buckle

   C without a buckle

   D full of buckles

5 You will find these safety tips are easily <u>doable</u>.

   A able to be done

   B not done

   C having done

   D mostly done

Root Words

CCSS

L.3.4c: Use a known root word as a clue to the meaning of an unknown word with the same root (e.g., *company, companion*).

Introduction Have you noticed that some words have the same parts? For example, the words *addition* and *additional* both have the **root word** *add*. This tells you that the words *addition* and *additional* are related to each other.

- Words with the same root have similar meanings.
- You can use a word you know to figure out the meaning of an unknown but related word.

> I visited my friend Kate. Her house has a new addition.
> Her family built the additional room for guests.

If you know that *add* means "to put together," you can figure out that *addition* means "something put together with something else," and *additional* means "extra" or "added."

Guided Practice **Read the sentence or sentences beside each number. Find and circle the word related to the underlined word. Then tell a partner the meaning of each word you circled.**

Hint

Think about the meaning of the word part that is the same in both words. Use the underlined word to help you figure out the meaning of the word you circled.

1. Kate's dog is her companion. He kept us <u>company</u> as we listened to the radio.

2. Suddenly, we heard the announcer make an <u>announcement</u>.

3. "Answer a question <u>correctly</u> and you'll win a ticket to the circus. Let me make a correction. You'll win two tickets!"

4. Then he asked, "Which inventor made an <u>invention</u> that lets you talk to someone who is far away?"

5. Kate called in with the answer. "The <u>scientist</u> Alexander Graham Bell made scientific discoveries and invented the telephone."

For numbers 1–4, use the underlined word in each sentence to help you answer each question.

1 Read the sentence below.

> You can <u>enter</u> the circus tent from Beach Street, but we used the **entrance** on Bay Road.

What does the word "entrance" mean as it is used in the sentence?

A a path

B a crosswalk

C a way to get into a place

D a way to leave a place

2 Read the sentence below.

> The seats in the tent were arranged in a <u>circle</u> around a **circular** stage.

What does the word "circular" mean as it is used in the sentence?

A strong

B round

C long

D raised

3 Read the sentence below.

> My ticket had a <u>number</u> that matched one of the **numerous** seats.

What does the word "numerous" mean as it is used in the sentence?

A lettered

B ordered

C few

D many

4 Read the sentence below.

> We watched dogs drive <u>bicycles</u> and a clown ride a **unicycle**.

What does the word "unicycle" mean as it is used in the sentence?

A a vehicle with one wheel

B a wagon pulled by dogs

C a clown car

D a small horse

Lesson 29
Using a Dictionary or Glossary

CCSS
L.3.4d: Use glossaries or beginning dictionaries, both print and digital, to determine or clarify the precise meaning of key words and phrases.

Introduction Many words have more than one meaning, or **definition**. You can use a dictionary or a glossary to check the exact meaning of a word or a phrase.

- A **dictionary** lists words in alphabetical order. Each entry gives the pronunciation, the part of speech, and the meaning of the word.

> **plant** (plănt) *n.* 1. a seedling 2. a factory *v.* 3. to put seeds or seedlings into the ground to grow 4. to set firmly in place: *Lee plants four stakes in the soil to mark the corners of his garden.*

> When there is more than one meaning, each definition is numbered.

> A sample sentence can make a word's meaning clearer.

- A **glossary** is like a dictionary. It is an alphabetical list of vocabulary words in a book. Each entry explains the meaning of a word as it is used in that book.

> **pest** (pĕst) 1. a plant or an animal that causes a problem: *Flies can be pests at a picnic.* 2. an annoying person

To find the right meaning of a word, first read all the definitions. Then see which meaning makes sense in the sentence you are reading.

Guided Practice Read the passage. Use the dictionary and glossary entries above to find the meaning of each underlined word. Then write the number of the definition above the word.

Hint

Ask yourself how the underlined word is used. Is it a noun? Is it a verb? Then reread the sentence using the definition you chose. Does the definition make sense?

After you <u>plant</u> flowers in your garden, you care for them. You

<u>plant</u> poles in the ground to support any tall stems. You love your

garden, but so do beetles! Some beetles eat <u>plants</u>. Try putting a

birdhouse in your garden to attract birds. Many birds will eat <u>pests</u>,

such as beetles.

Use the dictionary entries to answer numbers 1–4.

---

gather (găTH ur) *v.* **1.** to come together in a group **2.** to pick **3.** to conclude **4.** to collect information

1 Which definition matches how <u>gather</u> is used in this sentence?

In the morning, crows gather in the pumpkin patch.

A Definition 1

B Definition 2

C Definition 3

D Definition 4

---

probe (prōb) *n.* **1.** a thin tool used by doctors and dentists **2.** a search   *v.* **3.** to search or explore **4.** to get information about a person or thing

2 Which definition matches how <u>probe</u> is used in this sentence?

One crow uses its beak to probe the soil.

A Definition 1

B Definition 2

C Definition 3

D Definition 4

---

spot (spŏt) *n.* **1.** a stain or mark **2.** a place or location   *v.* **3.** to mark with dots **4.** to notice or see

3 Which definition matches how <u>spot</u> is used in this sentence?

The crow finds a juicy grub in one spot and swallows it.

A Definition 1

B Definition 2

C Definition 3

D Definition 4

---

4 Which definition matches how <u>spot</u> is used in this sentence?

The other crows spot many beetles chewing the pumpkin plants and quickly eat the beetles.

A Definition 1

B Definition 2

C Definition 3

D Definition 4

Lesson 30
Literal and Nonliteral Meanings

CCSS

L.3.5a: Distinguish the literal and nonliteral meanings of words and phrases in context (e.g., *take steps*).

Introduction Words and phrases often have more than one meaning.

- Sometimes words and phrases mean exactly what they say. For example, the words *took steps* can mean "walked" or "stepped."

> The hungry lion took steps toward the baby elephant.

- Sometimes words and phrases have a meaning that is different from their usual meaning. The words *took steps* can also mean "took action" or "acted."

> The mother elephant quickly took steps to protect her baby.

When you read, keep in mind that words or phrases might have more than one meaning. Use what you know and nearby words to figure out what the writer really means.

Guided Practice **Read each sentence. Circle the meaning of the underlined word or phrase.**

Hint

To figure out what the underlined part means, think about the words that come before and after it.

1 A tired elephant calf <u>drops off</u> after playing all morning.

    goes to sleep   **lets go**   **falls down**

2 A lion creeps through tall grass and <u>goes after</u> the calf.

    bothers   **follows**   **tries to get**

3 The mother elephant <u>trumpets</u> for help.

    asks   **makes a loud sound**   **plays the trumpet**

4 The calf wakes up but <u>freezes</u> when it sees the lion.

    turns to ice   **gets cold**   **is so scared it can't move**

For numbers 1–5, read each sentence. Then choose the correct meaning of each underlined word or phrase.

1 Many adult elephants <u>turn up</u> to protect the calf.

  A hold their trunks up

  B look toward the sky

  C look toward the calf

  D arrive suddenly

2 These smart <u>giants</u> use their tusks to protect the calf.

  A grown-up elephants

  B important animals

  C large monsters

  D huge people

3 The elephants <u>cut the lion off</u> each time he tries to dash between them.

  A remove a part of the lion

  B keep the lion from other lions

  C block the lion's way

  D stop the lion from roaring

4 The lion <u>takes off</u> when he realizes he can't catch the calf.

  A flies

  B leaves

  C jumps up

  D becomes angry

5 The lion doesn't want to <u>go another round</u> with the elephants.

  A give up

  B walk in a loop

  C run in a circle

  D fight again

Lesson 31
Real-Life Connections

CCSS
L.3.5b: Identify real-life connections between words and their use (e.g., describe people who are *friendly* or *helpful*).

Introduction When reading, you can connect the words on the page to your own life or to the wider world. Connecting words with real-life events can make their meaning clearer.

- What do you think of when you read the word *friendly*? You might remember a time when a friendly classmate smiled at you.

> A friendly classmate smiled and said, "Hi."

- When you think about the word *friendly*, you might also remember what friendly people and animals in your town or city have done.

> A friendly lady in town gives neighbors vegetables from her garden.
>
> Friendly dogs wag their tails and want to be patted.

Guided Practice Circle the correct words to complete each sentence. Then work with a partner to think of more ways to complete each sentence.

Hint

To help think of more ways to complete each sentence, ask your partner questions like these.

- When were you helpful?

- What do you do when you are curious about something?

1 A helpful person might _____ .

do chores   **break a glass**   **trip and fall**

2 If a person is curious, she might _____ .

go to sleep   **read a book**   **wrap a gift**

3 It would be selfish to _____ .

take all the toys   **give presents**   **help others**

4 A student could interrupt a class by _____ .

writing a story   **doing math**   **talking loudly**

For numbers 1–5, choose the correct answer to each question.

1 How might a **patient** person act?

A tell a friend to hurry up

B run to be first in line

C refuse to wait for someone

D teach a baby something new

2 What might a **stubborn** person say?

A "I like this new food after all."

B "I won't eat that even if it's good for me."

C "I agree with you about that."

D "I'll stay home because you need my help."

3 What might a **generous** person do?

A help a friend with homework

B eat candy without sharing

C disobey his parents

D scare a friend's dog

4 How might someone cause **confusion**?

A by solving a problem

B by telling the truth

C by giving poor directions

D by speaking clearly

5 What is a **rude** thing to do?

A invite a friend to a party

B talk while others are talking

C offer to wash the dishes

D help a neighbor plant a garden

Lesson 32
Shades of Meaning

CCSS
L.3.5c: Distinguish shades of meaning among related words that describe states of mind or degrees of certainty (e.g., *knew*, *believed*, *suspected*, *heard*, *wondered*).

Introduction Some words have similar definitions, but there are small differences in their meanings. These small differences are called **shades of meaning**.

- Think about the words *surprised* and *shocked*. They mean almost the same thing, but *shocked* has a stronger, or more forceful, meaning than *surprised* does.

> Max was surprised that so many people entered the poster contest.
>
> Max was shocked that so many people entered the poster contest.

- Look at the words below. They have similar definitions but different shades of meaning. They are arranged in order from the mildest meaning to the strongest.

> surprised ⟶ amazed ⟶ stunned ⟶ shocked

Guided Practice Complete each sentence by circling the word with the **strongest meaning.**

Hint

Read each sentence using the four answer choices. Think about which word gives the sentence the most forceful feeling.

1 Max _____ that the judges would like his poster.

    thought   **believed**   **knew**   **guessed**

2 His artwork was _____ .

    nice   **great**   **good**   **fine**

3 Max felt _____ when mud splashed on it.

    worried   **upset**   **unhappy**   **angry**

4 He was _____ that the mud wiped off easily.

    excited   **glad**   **happy**   **pleased**

For numbers 1–5, read each sentence. Then replace the underlined word by choosing the word with the strongest meaning.

1 Max was <u>worried</u> that his poster might not win a prize.

   A concerned

   B bothered

   C troubled

   D alarmed

2 He was <u>anxious</u> when his little brother walked toward the poster.

   A nervous

   B worried

   C panicky

   D uneasy

3 His little brother's hands were <u>dirty</u>!

   A filthy

   B muddy

   C soiled

   D stained

4 It would be <u>tough</u> to win a prize with a messy poster.

   A difficult

   B hard

   C rough

   D impossible

5 Max <u>supposed</u> his brother would not hurt his poster.

   A imagined

   B believed

   C felt

   D thought

Lesson 33
Words for Time and Space

CCSS

L.3.6: Acquire and use accurately grade-appropriate . . . words and phrases, including those that signal spatial and temporal relationships (e.g., *After dinner that night we went looking for them*).

Introduction How can you help make your writing clear for readers? One way is to use words and phrases that explain when and where actions or events take place.

- Words and phrases that tell *when* show the time events happen or the order in which they happen. *First, second, next, often, at noon*, and *in the morning* are some words and phrases that tell when events happen.

When	Plan your garden in the winter.
	First, decide what to grow.

- Words and phrases that tell *where* show the position or direction of something. *Down, around, under, close to*, and *on the right* are some words and phrases that tell where.

Where	Vegetables grow best in sunny areas.
	Some flowers can grow under trees or climb up walls.

Guided Practice Complete each sentence. If the parentheses ( ) say *when*, add a word or phrase that tells *when*. If they say *where*, add a word or phrase that tells *where*.

Hint

Think about what happens when you plant and care for a garden. What words and phrases that tell *when* or *where* will make the steps clear?

1 _____ , get a shovel and loosen the soil. (when)

2 Plant your seeds, and be sure to water them _____

_____ . (when)

3 The roots of the tiny seedlings will grow _____

_____ . (where)

4 The stems and leaves will grow _____

_____ . (where)

5 Don't forget to weed your garden _____

_____ . (when)

For numbers 1–5, complete each sentence by choosing the word or phrase that tells *when* or *where*.

1 If you have packets of seeds, _____ read the directions.

A slowly

B first

C carefully

D you must

2 It's a good idea to plant _____.

A vegetables

B many seeds

C in the morning

D with a friend

3 You can grow corn, squash, and beans _____.

A near one another

B if you want

C for food

D for your family

4 Some seeds sprout _____.

A in just a few days

B with little water

C but others do not

D without much trouble

5 Once your vegetables grow, you can share them _____.

A with neighbors

B easily

C too

D at school